SERAFINA'S STORIES

SERAFINA'S STORIES

RUDOLFO ANAYA

UNIVERSITY OF NEW MEXICO PRESS ❧ ALBUQUERQUE

10 09 08 07 06 05 04   1 2 3 4 5 6 7 8 9

Library of Congress Cataloging-in-Publication Data

Anaya, Rudolfo A.
  Serafina's stories / Rudolfo Anaya.
      p. cm.
  ISBN 0-8263-3569-1 (cloth : alk. paper)
  1. New Mexico—History—To 1848—Fiction. 2. Pueblo Revolt, 1680—Fiction.
3. Women storytellers—Fiction. 4. Pueblo Indians—Fiction. 5. Pueblo
women—Fiction. 6. Storytelling—Fiction. 7. Prisoners—Fiction. I. Title.
  PS3551.N27S44 2004
  813'.54—dc22
                          2004011783

Design and composition by Melissa Tandysh

Table of Contents

ONE

One gray January afternoon in 1680 the Governor of New Mexico stepped out of his residence in the Villa de Santa Fé. He was greeted by a gust of bitter cold wind that swept across the plaza. The Governor shivered and pulled his coat tightly around him.

"Another miserable day in this miserable kingdom," he muttered to himself.

He stood looking across the plaza, the common area surrounded by his residence and the other administrative buildings. The compound was well protected against attacks by Apaches. It could only be entered through guarded gates.

Outside this heart of the villa lay the homes of the Spanish and Mexican residents of Santa Fé. Today the low-lying adobe huts hugged the earth, sheltering their inhabitants from the January freeze.

A solitary man leading a burro laden with firewood came through a gate and made his way over the ruts of frozen mud. The man glanced at the Governor, barely nodded a greeting, then disappeared.

Throughout the villa feathers of thin, blue smoke rose from fireplace chimneys. Women were preparing supper for their families. Those who did not have urgent business outside their homes did not venture into the icy cold.

The Governor sighed. Such misery. In winter the cold kept the citizens of Santa Fé prisoners in their homes; in the summer they tried to eke out a living from their fields and from the sheep they pastured in the mountains. The Spaniards and the Pueblo Indians who worked for them were good pastores, and flocks of sheep had become a way of life in la Nueva México.

But recently the threat posed by dissident Pueblo Indians of the Río Grande worried the Governor. He dreaded the thought of the Pueblos turning against the Spanish colony.

Also, the Governor felt lonely. His wife had died the year before. The climate and the harsh way of life were most difficult for the women. And since there had been no children, the Governor felt adrift.

He gave up entertaining in his residence. La casa real, as it was called, was a long, single-story adobe building with vigas holding up a roof of latillas and mud. Melting snow soaked through the cracks, making it difficult for the small fireplaces to keep the rooms warm.

Not even the recent Christmas festivities had brought any relief to the Governor's mood. He spent his days taking care of his horses, riding in the hills, and, when necessary, leading his soldiers to settle disputes at the Indian pueblos from Isleta to Taos.

Lately there were more and more rumblings of discontent from the Pueblo Indians. Complaints came in on a daily basis. Rumors of revolution were in the air. The Governor did what he could to keep the peace between the Spanish settlers and the Pueblos, for he was entrusted with the safety of the colony.

The Governor's stomach growled. In the kitchen doña Ofelia, his housekeeper, an Indian woman from Picuris, was making supper. The aroma of the corn tortillas filled the house, mingling with the rich fragrances of venison stew and chile that bubbled in pots hung at the huge kitchen fireplace. She would prepare sweet natillas for dessert.

At the evening meal he allowed himself a glass of wine. He had to conserve his meager store of wine so it would last until the spring caravan of supplies came from New Spain, the land that lay south of the Río Grande.

The caravans from Chihuahua and Durango were the only connection the New Mexico colony had with Nueva España. Waiting for the spring caravan became a way of life for the denizens of Santa Fé.

Every year the people eagerly awaited the news the carts pulled by oxen and burros would bring from Mexico City, the once great capital of the Aztecs. Would the Viceroy send the additional troops the Governor had requested? The need for soldiers to protect Santa Fé weighed heavy on the Governor's mind as he stared across the empty, forlorn plaza.

That morning a few men had made their way out of the villa into the hills to gather firewood. Those who still had candles made from buffalo tallow might have one burning on the rough wood table where they ate supper. Otherwise the corner fireplace was the only source of light and warmth. During the long nights families sat huddled close to the fire listening to cuentos, the folktales the Spaniards had brought with them from Spain.

With the ground frozen, there was no work to do in the fields. Even the river was frozen solid, and boys spent long hours carrying blocks of ice home to melt for drinking water. Indian women, those taken as slaves from the Plains, cleaned the brick floors that were constantly tracked with mud. They ground corn and made tortillas. Pots of meat and beans simmered at every fireplace.

In a corral behind the Governor's residence a horse whinnied. Thank God only the most trusted natives had horses, the Governor thought. If all the Pueblos had horses, they would be a formidable enemy, and if they had the harquebuses, the Spanish rifles, a rebellion would mean the end of the colony.

The Governor shivered again. He knew he could not defend Santa Fé against an uprising by the Pueblos if they had horses and firearms. As it was, the constant attacks by the Apaches seemed to grow in number and audacity.

In 1598 the Spaniards, the Castillos, had come north to settle New Mexico, the tierra adentro. They settled near Española at San Gabriel. There don Juan de Oñate established the first capital, which Governor don Pedro de Peralta moved to Santa Fé in 1610. The Franciscan friars who accompanied the colonists came on a mission, to baptize the natives and teach them the Catholic faith.

The Españoles and the native Pueblo people learned to share many things, but the gulf between the European and native cultures remained great. Over the years those differences became deep-held animosities. According to Spanish law, the Governor of New Mexico had the right to collect corn and blankets from the natives. And he could force them to work, building churches, roads, and irrigation ditches, and preparing land for farming.

The Indians complained about the harsh rule of the Castillos. They were paid a pittance, and the work often lasted into their own farming season. The friars also used Pueblo laborers to build mission churches. Thousands of natives had been converted into the Catholic religion. The Governor knew the natives suffered the long winters, but there was little he could do.

Religion lay at the heart of the animosity between the Spaniards and the natives. The Spaniards were Catholics; the mission of the friars was conversion. But the Pueblo Indians had their own religion. For centuries they had worshipped in the way of their ancestors.

The Spanish friars branded the Pueblos' religion paganism, destroyed their religious objects, and forbade them to hold their Kachina dances. The Pueblos resisted. From time to time they struck back, threatening the friars, sometimes killing those in the outlying pueblos. Then the Governor had to ride out with his soldiers and punish those responsible.

The Spaniards were vastly outnumbered by the Pueblo Indians, so no dissent could be allowed. At the first sign of unrest the Governor would send his soldiers to arrest the dissidents. In this way, the Governor thought, he could assure the safety of his colony.

The month of January dawned with fresh snow covering the high peaks of the Sierra Madre that towered over the villa. January also brought what the Spaniards feared most: secret plans for an uprising had been discovered. A Pueblo Indian loyal to the Spaniards had warned that a group of natives were preparing for war. He named twelve conspirators.

The Governor had acted quickly. Three days ago he had sent one of his captains, Cristóbal Anaya, to the northern pueblos to arrest those accused of plotting war. Even as the Governor pondered this recent action, a sentry stationed at the far end the plaza called, informing him that the detail was returning, leading prisoners.

The sentry's cry created a stir. A few hardy men left their homes to see the rebel Indians who had been captured. Women whose husbands or sons had gone with the arrest party were eager to learn if they had returned safely. Wrapped in buffalo robes, the denizens of la Villa Real de la Santa Fé gathered in the dusk to watch as the prisoners were marched into the plaza.

The twelve Indians walked with hands bound, faces downcast. The soldiers on horseback tugged at the ropes, urging the prisoners to hurry forward. The captives were led through the gate and across the plaza to face the Governor.

"Your Excellency," Capitán Anaya shouted. "I wish to report the capture and delivery of twelve prisoners. All of my men have returned safely."

A cheer went up from the crowd. Women crossed their foreheads. Men nodded their approval.

"Well done, capitán," the Governor replied, glancing at the prisoners. A sorry lot. Clothed in buckskin with wool blankets around their shoulders to ward off the cold, they stood in silence. "Lock them up. I will question them after dinner."

The soldiers led the Indians to the jail, and those who had gathered to watch sighed with relief. All the soldiers had returned safely; that was what mattered. They would hear the tale of the adventure during supper. People quickly disappeared back into the warmth of their homes.

Two men with a dead deer strung on a pole between them crossed the plaza; then all was quiet in the dusk of evening.

The Governor, too, retreated into his residence to eat a quiet dinner, alone. He felt mixed emotions. On the one hand, those plotting insurrection had been caught, but he also knew he would have to deal harshly with them. They had to be taught a lesson, a lesson that would not be lost on others who might conspire to revolt.

After dinner the Governor summoned his secretary and notary, don Alfonso, and his captains to his office. Don Alfonso was one of the few men in the villa who could write. As Capitán Anaya gave his report the secretary wrote furiously, recording every detail. The twelve accused had been apprehended at six of the northern pueblos. There were loud protests from the prisoners' families and neighbors, but there had been no armed resistance.

The Governor thanked the captain and ordered the Indians brought in, so their names and the charges against them could be entered into the record.

When the prisoners were gathered in the office, the secretary asked them if they spoke Spanish. All nodded. He then proceeded to read the charges against them, warning them of the seriousness of each indictment. Charges of insurrection against a colony of the King of Spain were punishable by life imprisonment, or by death.

Everyone present in the dimly lit room remembered that the first governor of New Mexico had ordered one foot cut off each of twenty-four Indians from Acoma Pueblo who had attacked Spanish soldiers. Many Acoma women and children had been sold into slavery.

A chill permeated the small room. One by one each prisoner stepped forward and gave his baptismal Spanish name. The Governor looked up in surprise when the twelfth prisoner responded "me llamo Serafina."

Both the Governor and the secretary looked closely at the prisoner, as did the guards.

"Did you say Serafino?" the secretary asked.

"No, Serafina." The voice was that of a woman.

In the dim light cast by the burning candles the Governor realized the prisoner was a young woman.

"Remove your manta," he ordered.

The young woman removed the blanket that had covered her head and shoulders, letting loose a cascade of long, black hair that spilled over her shoulders.

The Governor stood. "Capitán. Did you know this prisoner was a woman?"

"No, Your Excellency," the captain sputtered. "The prisoners were bound and brought in as you see them now. Because of the cold I allowed some to keep their blankets. As you can see—"

"No matter," the Governor interupted. "We must proceed." He looked at the prisoners. "You have heard the charges read against you. You are accused of conspiring to incite revolution. This is a serious threat. If the charges prove right, you will be accused of treason against His Most Royal Majesty."

The prisoners stood with heads bowed, saying nothing. The Governor's captains understood the severity of the situation. If these leaders of the insurrection were not punished, tomorrow there would be new plans to revolt against Spanish rule. And tomorrow and tomorrow. The Governor was right. The leaders of this rebellious plot had to be dealt with harshly.

"What do you suggest?" the Governor asked don Alfonso.

"There are two possibilities," the secretary answered. "Each man could be sentenced to die. That is the most severe punishment of the law. Or each man could be flogged publicly in the plaza and sold into slavery. That would be the least severe punishment."

A shudder passed through the Indian prisoners. They did not fear death or a public whipping. What they feared was being sold as slaves to work the mines of Zacatecas, never to see their families again, never to see their sacred homeland again. For them, this punishment was worse than death.

The Governor looked at Serafina. Even exhausted and muddied as she was, she kept her poise. She was the only one looking directly at him. Putting her to death would not be one of his options.

He turned to the secretary. "Should the prisoners be tried individually or as a group?"

"I suggest we try them one by one," the secretary replied. "In that way the natives from the pueblos who come to attend the trials can report each day back to their pueblos on the proceedings."

"Very well," the Governor said. "We will try the first prisoner tomorrow morning." He turned to a young captain, Capitán Márquez, who had spent a year in the university at Salamanca. "Capitán Márquez, you will act as attorney for the prisoners."

"Yes, Your Excellency," the captain replied.

"Very well. We assemble tomorrow in the portal. Take the prisoners back to the jail."

As the prisoners were led out of the room the Governor stopped Serafina.

"You are too young to be plotting revolution," he said.

"I am my father's helper," she replied.

"Ah, so you follow your father's guidance. His name did not appear on our list. Will he come to attend the trial?"

"Now that you have taken us prisoners, none of the elders will come to speak to you. Trust has been broken."

"I see," said the Governor. "You speak Spanish very well. Who taught you?"

"I was brought up in the mission church by the friars."

"And still you plotted with the men against our rule?"

"What you call a plot was a gathering of elders from the different pueblos. We met to discuss how our people suffer this winter. We were ready to send a delegation to meet with you to discuss how little corn we have left and how few buffalo robes."

The Governor was surprised by the young woman's calm. Normally the Indians looked at the ground when they addressed a Spanish officer, but this girl looked directly into his eyes. She was fearless.

"Do you believe in God?"

"Yes."

"Then you cannot believe in pagan gods."

"They are my ancestral gods," Serafina answered. "They all live together—"

"Nonsense!" the Governor scoffed, advancing on the girl until he loomed over her, a threatening presence.

Serafina stood her ground.

"Heresy," the secretary muttered.

The Governor turned and looked at don Alfonso, who had been recording the proceedings. "Enough," he said. "Leave the room."

The old man wrinkled his brow, then picking up his quill, ink well, and papers he hurried out.

The Governor looked at the girl. He realized that beneath the day's grime and fatigue stood a young woman no older than fifteen.

"Sit down," the Governor commanded, and he too sat. He stared at the girl and she at him. "Do you know what will happen to you for joining those plotting against His Majesty's rule?"

"I will be made a slave," she replied.

"Yes," said the Governor, leaning forward on his desk. "I have to make an example of you and your fellow rebels. Each of you will be flogged in public, then sent as slaves to the mines in Zacatecas."

Even in the dim candlelight the Governor saw a shadow cross the girl's face for the first time.

"Separated from our families," she whispered.

"Yes. If I do not punish you severely others will follow in your footsteps. My people depend on me for their safety."

"And the cruelest punishment is to send us away from our homes, our sacred earth?"

The Governor nodded. He knew how much the circle of the pueblo meant to the natives. It was their universe. To be ostracized from community and family was a punishment far worse than death.

Yes, the Governor knew what it meant to be driven from one's homeland. He, too, had been sent away—to this miserable northern kingdom to govern an unruly settlement, to deal with friars who constantly disobeyed him, and to safeguard colonists who often complained of his rule.

"The first man will be tried tomorrow," the Governor said, returning to his seat. He was tired. The knowledge of what he had to do weighed heavily on him. He wished there were a way out of the predicament—something he could trade for the allegiance of the natives.

For a long time they sat in silence until Serafina spoke.

"You are a prisoner, like us."

"What?" the Governor responded. He laughed. "Me, a prisoner? That's ridiculous."

Then the smile left his face. Did the girl have the ability to read his mind? He had heard that some of the natives possessed the gift of divination.

"Are you one of those we call brujos?" he asked.

A faint smile crossed her lips. "No, I am a storyteller."

"Do you know our cuentos?"

"Yes. When your people visit our pueblo they tell stories. My mother has learned many, and she taught them to me."

"I love a good story," mused the Governor. "I read the few books that I can have shipped to me from Spain. But there is no substitute for a good story. Let's see how clever you are. Tell me one."

"I will, for a price."

"Ah, you *sell* your stories! Very well, what is the price?"

"If you like my story you must free the man you plan to try tomorrow."

"Free the prisoner? Nonsense."

"But you cannot lose the wager," she said. "If you don't like the story you don't set him free."

The Governor chuckled. The winter nights were long, and for ages, it seemed, he had not been able to sleep.

"My mother used to tell me stories when I was a child," he mused. "Her voice lulled me to sleep."

He stopped himself. This was ridiculous. He should not speak this way in front of a native.

"All right. I agree. Tell me a story, and if I like it I will free your fellow prisoner tomorrow."

Again he chuckled. How could he lose? Perhaps the girl knew the cuentos, but it took a special talent to make the old stories come alive.

"It's a bargain," Serafina said, and she began her story.

TWO

Juan del Oso

A long time ago in the village of Questa there lived a man and his wife. They had a lovely daughter whose name was Aida. Many young men came to court her, but her parents guarded her carefully. Each day they took her to the fields to tend the corn, beans, and chile they grew.

The village of Questa was located at the foot of high, rugged mountains. Bears sometimes came down from the sierra to eat elotes, the tender corn. The father warned Aida to be careful because he had seen the tracks of a large bear nearby.

One day when her parents were busy with other tasks, Aida went to the garden alone. She was picking corn when suddenly a giant bear appeared. Before she could scream or run, the bear picked her up and carried her to his cave in the mountain.

The bear didn't harm Aida. To be quite truthful, he fell in love with her. So he decided to keep her prisoner in his cave. Each day when the bear left in search of food, he would block the entrance with a gigantic boulder. In this way Aida could not escape.

Aida's parents searched everywhere for her, but they couldn't find her. After some time they stopped looking for her and resigned themselves to their loss.

That spring Aida gave birth to a son. She baptized him Juan del Oso, John of the Bear.

Juan grew quickly, and by the time he was a year old he could talk. By the time he was two, he was six feet tall. Aida was happy with her son. By the time he was six she had taught him spelling and numbers, and she had told him stories about her home and her parents. They were Juan's grandparents, and she wished they could see their grandson.

—Why can't we visit them? Juan asked one day.

—Bear puts a boulder at the entrance each time he leaves. We cannot move it.

—Oh yes I can, Juan said. He went straight to the entrance, leaned against the heavy boulder, and easily moved it aside.

Juan and his mother ran quickly out of the cave and down the mountain. They were nearing her parents home when they heard grunting and growling behind them. It was Bear!

He will punish us for escaping, thought Juan. I must save my mother.

—Go on! he shouted and turned to meet an angry Bear.

Juan and the Bear fought a tremendous battle. Tall pine trees fell as they struggled. Boulders crashed from the mountain top. Finally Juan was able to kill Bear.

He ran to his mother and together they went to her parents' home. The old man and woman were overjoyed to have their daughter back, and delighted they now had a grandson.

That fall they sent Juan to school, but he was so big the children made fun of him. Juan picked up six boys and threw them against a wall, breaking a few of their bones. The parents of the boys complained, and Juan could no longer attend school.

—I must go and seek my fortune, he said. Make me a sheepherder's staff so I may tend sheep.

Forty men cut down the tallest pine tree they could find and shaped the staff. Groaning under the weight they carried it to Juan. He picked it up with one hand.

Juan said goodbye to his mother and grandparents and set off. As he walked he saw a buffalo. He killed it with one blow of his staff and had it for a meal.

Later Juan met a man by the side of a river. The man carried a huge shovel in one hand.

—Who are you? asked Juan.

—I am Moves Rivers, the man replied.

—I am Juan del Oso. Why don't we travel together?

—Very well, said Moves Rivers. But I am the leader.

—You can be the leader if you can lift my staff.

Moves Rivers tried to lift Juan's staff but he couldn't. Then Juan picked up Moves Rivers's shovel and with one scoop he made the Río Grande.

—You are stronger, Moves Rivers said. You be the leader.

They walked on until they met another giant of a man who carried a pick.

—Who are you? asked Juan.

—I am Moves Mountains.

—You can come with us if you can lift my shepherd's staff, said Juan.

Moves Mountains tried to lift the huge staff but couldn't. Then Juan took the pick, stuck it in the ground, and created the Sangre de Cristo Mountains.

—You are the leader, Moves Mountains said reluctantly.

The three became thieves, stealing from the ox-drawn wagons that went from Santa Fé to Chihuahua.

One day Juan and Moves Mountains left Moves Rivers at their camp while they went hunting. He was to have supper ready when they returned later that day.

Moves Rivers cooked twenty buffalo for dinner and sat down to rest. Soon the Devil appeared, disguised as an old, gnarled dwarf. He kicked dirt on the food.

Moves Rivers jumped up to punish the dwarf, but the dwarf was so strong he gave Moves Rivers a beating and left him with a cracked skull.

When Juan and Moves Mountains returned they found their friend in a terrible state. They asked him what had happened.

—I climbed a tree to see if I could see you, he said. I fell and cracked my skull.

The next day it was Moves Mountains' turn to stay in camp and prepare dinner. He cooked twenty buffalo and sat down to rest. Along came the Devil disguised as an ancient man; he kicked dirt on the dinner.

An angry Moves Mountains accosted the Devil, but the Devil was so strong he gave the poor fellow a terrible beating.

When the two friends returned and asked what had happened, Moves Mountains said he, too, had climbed a pine tree and fallen.

The following day it was Juan's turn to stay in the camp. He was very hungry, so he cooked forty buffalo and lay down to rest. Shortly thereafter the Devil appeared and kicked dirt on the food. Juan grabbed the Devil, and a terrible fight ensued. Juan knocked the Devil down with his staff and tore off his ear. The Devil ran away, howling with pain.

Juan put the ear in his pocket and followed. He came to a large cave where the Devil disappeared inside. Juan peered into the cave and saw that it was very deep. Juan knew the Devil always hides a treasure in deep caverns. He returned to camp with a plan.

When the two friends arrived they accused Juan of running away from the dwarf.

Juan laughed and showed them the Devil's ear.

—Here's the pine tree you two climbed, he said, shaming his friends for lying.

He told them about the Devil's cave. The next day he bought a strong rope and a bell from some merchants passing through.

The three went to the cave and let down the rope with the bell tied at the end. Moves Rivers climbed down the rope, but a terrible wind forced him to ring the bell, and they pulled him out. Then Moves Mountains tried climbing down, but he too found the wind too strong and they pulled him out.

Finally Juan climbed down; his staff was so heavy the wind couldn't dash him against the rocks. He climbed safely to the floor of the cave.

Juan remembered his grandparents telling a story about a cave full of buried treasure. He thought he might find gold and other precious stones.

He came to a door and opened it. To his astonishment he found a beautiful young woman in the room.

—Who are you? he asked.

—I am the king's daughter, she replied. The Devil wanted my two sisters and me to marry his three sons, but my father refused. The Devil cast a spell on us and made us prisoners. The giant who guards my room will return at any moment. You must get away or he will kill you.

—I'm not afraid of giants, Juan replied.

At that moment the giant appeared. He was the most horrible creature imaginable. He grabbed at Juan but Juan was too swift. He gave the giant a blow with his shepherd's staff and killed him.

The young woman was overjoyed at being freed.

—You are my savior, she said. Now if only you could rescue my two sisters who are prisoners in the other rooms.

—I will, Juan said. But first I have to get you out of this cave. He tied the rope around her slim waist and rang the bell. Moves Rivers and Moves Mountains pulled her up. Imagine their surprise when they saw a lovely young woman at the end of the rope.

She told the two how Juan had killed the giant and was now rescuing her sisters. They should all wait there at the entrance to the cave to see if he was successful.

In the meantime Juan approached a second door sealed with a giant boulder. Juan easily moved it aside and met the second lovely sister.

—I freed your sister, Juan explained, and I will free you.

—You cannot. I am guarded by a tiger that sleeps in the cave. You must flee before he devours you!

At that moment the tiger awakened and rushed at Juan. Juan was so agile he sidestepped the tiger and gave it a blow with his staff, killing the fierce animal.

—Oh thank you, the young woman said. You are my savior. Now if you could only rescue our youngest sister. She is in a room guarded by a huge snake.

—First we must get you out of here, Juan said.

He took her to the rope and tied it around her waist. Then he rang the bell and Moves Rivers and Moves Mountains pulled her up. Imagine how delighted the two sisters were to be reunited outside the Devil's cave!

In the cave Juan found the third room. He forced open the heavy door and found the youngest sister. She was the most beautiful of the three, and the moment Juan saw her he fell in love with her.

—What is your name? he asked.

—I am Celestina, the youngest daughter of the king. Who are you and what are you doing here?

—I am Juan del Oso and I have come to free you from this evil enchantment.

—You must run away, she cried. A venomous serpent guards this room! It will kill you!

—I saved your two sisters, Juan replied, and I intend to save you.

A loud hiss filled the room as the huge snake uncoiled and struck at Juan. Juan jumped to the side and hit the snake with his staff. He froze with fear when he realized the serpent had seven heads, each with fangs that dripped with venom.

Juan said the prayer his mother had taught him, and that gave him the courage to fight. The serpent tried to wrap itself around Juan and suffocate him, but he kept striking at the heads until he had crushed each one.

When the serpent lay dead Celestina spoke.

—You have saved me and my sisters, she said. Now you must be rewarded. If you take us to our father, who is a great king, he will make you a rich man. And he will give one of us to you as a wife.

—That is a worthy prize, Juan replied. But he might ask for proof that I rescued you.

—Cut the tongue from each serpent head and take it to him, Celestina instructed.

—What else? asked Juan

—I give you my ring, she said. My father will recognize it and know you are my savior.

Juan put the serpents' tongues and the ring in the pocket that held the Devil's ear. Then he took Celestina to the rope, tied it around her waist, and rang the bell. Instantly Moves Rivers and Moves Mountains pulled her up.

When they saw they had three lovely young women who were the daughters of a king they decided to collect the reward for themselves and abandon Juan in the cave.

When Juan tied the rope around his waist and rang the bell nothing happened. His two friends had escaped with the three girls, leaving him a prisoner in the Devil's cave.

Many days and nights passed and Juan grew very hungry. He remembered the Devil's ear and thought he might eat it. He pulled the ear from his pocket.

—It's your fault I'm going to die in this cave, he said. He took a bite of the ear but it was very tough.

—You're not even good to eat! Juan shouted and threw the ear on the ground.

A puff of smoke exploded and the Devil appeared in the form of the dwarf Juan had followed to the cave days ago.

—Thank you for returning my ear to me, said the Devil. In return I will grant you three wishes.

—I want to be out of here, Juan commanded, and instantly he found himself outside the cave.

—I need food and water.

A table laden with food and jars of fresh water appeared before him. When he had eaten Juan asked the Devil what had happened to the girls he had rescued from the cave.

—Your two friends took the girls to their father the king. He had promised whoever found them could marry his daughters. The two eldest daughters are ready to marry your friends as we speak.

—Take me there, said Juan, and in a flash he found himself in a large reception hall where the wedding was about to take place.

Celestina instantly recognized Juan.

—Father! she cried. This is the man who rescued me from the cave.

—How can that be? responded the king. Have Moves Rivers and Moves Mountains lied to me?

—They have, she answered.

—Step forward, the king said to Juan. How is it you can appear from out of nowhere? What do you seek?

—My name is Juan del Oso, replied Juan, and I came to reclaim my honor. Moves Rivers and Moves Moutains lied to you. It was I who rescued your daughters from the Devil's cave. I killed the giant, the tiger, and the seven-headed serpent.

The wedding guests gasped in astonishment.

—Can you prove this? asked the king.

—Here are the seven tongues of the serpent, replied Juan, and he took the tongues from his pocket and threw them on the floor. And here is Celestina's ring.

—Yes, that is her ring, said the king, convinced that Juan had rescued his daughters and that Moves Rivers and Moves Mountains were impostors. He ordered his guards to lock them up.

—I beg you, wise king, give me Celestina for my wife, said Juan.

The king looked at his daughter.

—I accept this brave young man who rescued me from the evil spell, she replied. She took his hand.

They were married that same day. The king gave Juan half of his fortune. Later Juan and Celestina traveled in a splendid coach to visit his mother and grandparents. The entire town came out to greet them, for by now Juan's adventures were well known. Juan built a beautiful home there at the foot of Taos Mountain where perhaps they live today.

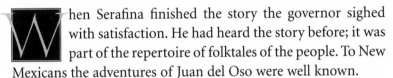

hen Serafina finished the story the governor sighed with satisfaction. He had heard the story before; it was part of the repertoire of folktales of the people. To New Mexicans the adventures of Juan del Oso were well known.

But he had never heard tales from such a spellbinding storyteller. Her tone, the rhythms in her voice, and her presence had allowed his mind to drift into the story. He felt he was there with Juan as he rescued the three princesses from their entrapment.

Storytelling was the principal entertainment for New Mexican families. Reciting cuentos from the vast storehouse of folktales was an art in which Serafina excelled. As he listened to her he felt the burdensome responsibility of being governor lifted. His eyelids had grown heavy as he relaxed and let his imagination carry him to the final scene at the castle.

"Very good," he muttered, "very good. You have a gift for storytelling."

He stood, went to the door, and called the guard.

"Gaspar," he said to the young man, "take the prison—" He paused. "Return Serafina to the stockade."

"Yes, Your Excellency," replied the guard. He led her out of the room, leaving a very relaxed Governor thinking how much he had enjoyed the story. He stumbled to his bed and slept a peaceful sleep.

The next morning the crowing of a rooster awakened the Governor. He got up, stretched, and looked around him.

"What a wonderful sleep," he said.

He recalled the events of the previous night. The Indian girl, Serafina, was a delightful storyteller. He hadn't slept so soundly in months.

Smiling and humming a simple tune, he washed and dressed, then ate his breakfast. He ate like a bear after a long winter's sleep.

He then went out to attend to the day's business. Already the prisoners were lined up under the portal. Don Alfonso, the secretary, had set up a small table on the frozen ground to record the proceedings; the officers stood nearby. Behind the prisoners it seemed the entire villa of Santa Fé had gathered to watch, the men stamping their feet on the frozen earth, the women pulling their tapalos tightly around their heads.

The Governor said good morning to his officers and sat next to don Alfonso. It was a bright and sunny day on the high plateau of Santa Fé. By noon the sun's warmth would lift the spirits of the paisanos. Women could wash and hang clothes out to dry; the men could replenish wood piles.

"I have made a list of the prisoners in the order they will be tried," whispered don Alfonso to the Governor.

"Thank you," said the Governor, looking at the list. "Place the girl at the end."

He looked at the prisoners until his eyes rested on Serafina. The wager! He had promised to free the man on trial if her story pleased him!

Now her gaze held his. Will you keep your promise? her eyes seemed to ask. But it was a silly bet. Surely he couldn't set one of the rebels free. There was a group of residents within the villa that didn't agree with his administration. They were friends of the governor he had replaced, a very wicked man. These enemies would call for his resignation if he set a prisoner free.

But the girl had won the bet. She had told a story that had not only entertained him, but had also brought a welcome rest.

And there was the matter of honor. A Spaniard's word was his honor, and he had given his word.

But he hadn't expected to lose. He had laughed at her when she said she would trade a story for the freedom of one of the prisoners.

"Your Excellency," the secretary whispered, breaking the spell that held the Governor. "It is time to proceed with the trial. Shall I read the charges?"

The Governor nodded.

"Will the prisoner known as Popé come forward," said the secretary. A dark, stocky man of about forty stepped out of the line.

"This man currently resides in the Pueblo of Taos. He is a known rabblerouser. Capitán Márquez will act as his attorney, but there is little defense to be offered. All twelve have been charged with plotting insurrection."

The Governor did not respond. He had returned his gaze to Serafina.

The secretary continued, turning to the captain who had been apppointed to offer a defense for the prisoners. "What say you, Capitán Márquez?"

Capitán Márquez cleared his throat and stepped forward. "I, Capitán Horacio Gómez Márquez, assigned to be guardian and defense attorney for the Indians, come to beg for clemency from Your Excellency. I have explained the charge against the prisoner through the interpreter, although I am sure the prisoner speaks or at least understands the Castillian language quite well. I have asked the prisoner to call witnesses on his behalf. He replies that he has no witnesses to call."

Here Capitán Márquez paused and looked in the direction of a group of Pueblo Indians huddled against a wall by the south side of the plaza. They had been allowed to enter the villa to witness the trial so that they could report the results of Spanish justice back to their pueblos.

It was not unusual for men from the various pueblos to come in and out of the villa during the day. Some came to trade, some to work for Fray Tomás at the church, some to see their wives, who worked in the homes of the Españoles.

Capitán Márquez spoke. "The Pueblos have sent representatives to report back to their elders, but none has stepped forward to testify for the prisoner."

The Governor cleared his throat. He had followed the gaze of the captain. "Well, if they have no witnesses in their defense, how does the man plead?"

Capitán Márquez remained silent for a moment. He had been assigned to defend the Indians, but they had been uncooperative. They claimed to have met as a group to discuss grievances they proposed to forward to the Governor.

"Well, I have little to say in defense of the prisoner. He is a known leader of those who speak of insurrection. According to our informant, who cannot be identified for his own safety, this group has gathered to plot an attack on our settlements."

"How reliable is the informant?" asked the Governor.

"As you know, Your Excellency, sometimes the information is true. But sometimes it is grounded in hearsay, or jealousies, or family feuds. One can never be sure."

"Very well, continue," said the Governor.

"Well, the natives complain that we have taken much corn and many blankets from them. They say they are suffering from the severe cold. If this can be proven to be true, and they assembled simply to petition the Governor, then I can only ask that Your Lordship show clemency."

Some in the crowd nodded; others shook their heads.

"Show no pity!" a man shouted.

Murmurs of dissent broke out.

"How would I show clemency?" asked the Governor, raising his hand to quiet the crowd.

"At best, don't banish the man to Mexico. Make him work in servitude for a year here in the villa."

Again some in the crowd raised their voices. Yes, a year's hard labor might cleanse thoughts of revolution from the prisoner.

The Governor looked at Serafina. Her bright eyes again reminded him of their wager. For a moment he felt confused. Had he really lost the bet last night?

"As I understand," said the Governor, "the evidence against this man is based on hearsay. It is the word of our informant against his. Is that true?"

Capitán Márquez nodded. "That is true, Your Excellency."

"Then what would be the greatest clemency we could offer the prisoner?"

The captain looked surprised. "I suppose it would be freedom. Allowing him to go back to his pueblo with a stern warning."

Voices in the crowd rose to agree with that solution. A minority shouted no. The prisoner must be made an example. He must be punished.

Having offered the only defense he could muster, Capitán Márquez stepped back.

The secretary cleared his throat and spoke. "That concludes the presentation of evidence, Your Excellency. You must pass sentence."

The Governor looked at his secretary and nodded. Pass sentence? Exile the man to the mines of Zacatecas? Separate him forever from his family?

Or let him go. Had the girl tricked him into the bet? No, she was a child, no older than fifteen. He had entered the transaction of his own accord.

To free the man would be looked on as an act of mercy. That was what was needed most in the relations between the Indians and the Spaniards, an act of mercy.

"We must be merciful," the Governor muttered. The secretary thought he hadn't heard correctly. Standing next to him, Fray Tomás nodded.

"Merciful?" the secretary repeated.

"Yes. I conclude the charges against this man have not been proven. As Capitán Márquez states, the charges are based on hearsay. I say we must set this man free."

He looked at Serafina and thought he saw a smile cross her lips. Some in the crowd nodded their assent. Yes, mercy should be shown. The Governor was right. In this way the natives would learn that there was forgiveness in the hearts of the Spanish settlers.

Others in the crowd disagreed. This was a time to punish those who plotted the overthrow of the colony. Mercy, bah! That would only show weakness.

"I'm afraid I don't understand," muttered the secretary. "Are you saying free the prisoner?"

The Governor stood. "Yes, free the prisoner."

"But Governor," one of the captains protested, "the man is a rebel. He is accused of planning our downfall."

"I am sure there are many who speak against our rule of law," the Governor responded. "Are we to banish every pueblo man from this land because he expresses his opinion? If I had evidence there was an actual plot that threatened the colony, I would be the first to stamp it out. And yes, punish the perpetrators. But in this case the evidence is lacking."

The Governor leaned and whispered to the secretary. "As for the other eleven prisoners, see that they are fed and allowed to bathe. Have doña Ofelia send the girl a clean dress to wear."

The Governor turned smartly and disappeared into his residence, leaving behind him the citizens of the villa arguing over his decision.

The prisoner, cut loose from his shackles, went quickly to his countrymen who had come to observe the trial. As a group they quietly disappeared through one of the gates leading out of the plaza. Soon all the northern pueblos would know what had happened that morning.

As for the residents of the villa, they would argue all day and deep into the night, debating the Governor's verdict. Some argued that it was a good gesture of friendship toward their neighbors, others saw it as an expression of weakness. Still others thought the Governor had gone out of his mind.

All asked, What will he do tomorrow when the second prisoner is tried?

The Governor paid no attention to the turmoil he had created. He went about his business with renewed energy, inspecting the troops and in the afternoon supervising the cleaning of the horse corrals. That evening he ate a hearty supper, read the secretary's prodeedings of the trial, then thought of going to bed.

But he wasn't sleepy. When the spring caravans travelled south, the Viceroy would learn he had freed the prisoner. The Governor had his enemies not only in Santa Fé but in Mexico City.

A pox on my enemies, he thought. I did what I thought as right.

The girl, he thought. Last night's story had been such a delight. Did he dare tempt fate again? Why not? Listening to a story was far preferable to sitting in his office and reading the adventures of Don Quixote late into the night.

He rose, lit a candle, and made his way to his office. Gaspar, the sentry, stood guard outside. The Governor instructed him to bring the girl to the office.

"The storyteller," the young guard said. The night before he had listened at the door and heard the girl telling the story of Juan del Oso.

"Yes, the storyteller," the Governor said.

Minutes later, when the guard led Serafina into his office, the Governor was astounded by her beauty. She wore a white cotton dress, and her long black hair shimmered as it fell over the clean wool blanket doña Ofelia had provided. For a moment she reminded him of his wife, a woman of dark complexion with black hair. With a twinge of sadness he thought of their life together and the children they had never had.

"Thank you, Gaspar," said the Governor, dismissing the guard. "Come in by the fire," he said to Serafina and drew her into the room and to a chair near the huge fireplace.

"Have you been treated well?" he asked.

"Yes, Your Excellency. Doña Ofelia is very kind."

"It's late. Did I disturb your sleep?"

"No, Your Excellency. The sun has just set. It isn't late."

"Here, the entire villa goes to sleep after dinner. Perhaps it's different in your pueblo."

"We also follow the rhythms of the sun," replied Serafina.

"Well, candles are expensive," said the Governor, motioning toward the candles that provided light in his office.

"Thank you for releasing the prisoner," she said.

"Yes. Well, we made a bargain, I kept my word. Besides, there are certain political advantages to be gained from my action. And your story was like a good medicine I needed. But the medicine doesn't last."

"Perhaps you need another story," Serafina said.

"And the wager is the same?"

"Yes. If the story pleases you, you free a prisoner?"

The Governor smiled. Perhaps it was not the magic of the young woman's storytelling that had allowed him to rest last night. Perhaps he had already decided to release the first prisoner, to help bind the wounds between the Spanish settlers and the natives. Well, tonight he would find out.

"Very well," he said.

He took the large chair opposite her and Serafina began her story.

FOUR

Miranda's Gift

Miranda lived with her father, don Ezequiel, in a large and comfortable house near the banks of the Pecos River. Don Ezequiel was a merchant who was often away on business, so Miranda spent much time alone.

Her closest neighbors were the widow doña Benina and her daughter, Petra. The widow and her daughter were very poor, and Miranda often took them gifts of food. One day when Miranda was visiting them, doña Benina took her aside.

—You're fifteen now, and you don't have a mother to take care of you—no one to comb your hair and teach you the things young women need to know. If your father married me, I would be like a mother to you.

Miranda mentioned this to her father, and he thought it was a good idea. He married doña Benina, and on the day of the wedding he gave Miranda a calf. To the stepsister, Petra, he gave a goat.

Doña Benina planned a big party. She invited all the neighbors. Then she pressured don Ezequiel to kill Miranda's calf for the feast.

To please his new wife he killed the calf. Then he sent Miranda to the river to wash the stomach and intestines. When the tripe was washed, they would cook it with hominy to make a stew of menudo.

Sadly, Miranda went to the river, and as she was washing the tripe a large gold fish rose out of the water and grabbed it. The fish swam away with it.

Miranda ran along the bank, crying. She knew her stepmother would punish her for the loss. Finally exhausted, she sat down to rest.

—Dear Virgin, please help me.

As she was praying a woman appeared. Miranda looked up to see the kindest face she had ever seen. The woman wore a plain dress and a blue serape covered her shoulders.

—Why are you crying, my daughter? she asked softly.

Miranda explained what had happened.

—I can help you, said the woman. Walk farther down the river. There you will find a hut with an old man on a bed, a child in his cradle, and a pot with food on the stove. Beat the old man with a broom and throw him out of the hut. Spank the child and throw dirt on the pot of beans. Spread ashes throughout the house. When you have done this look in the bucket on the table and there you will find the tripe you lost.

Miranda was surprised this beautiful woman would tell her to do such dreadful things, but she went down the river until she found the hut.

She went in and found the old man and the child.

I can't beat this old man and spank this innocent child, she thought. I have been taught to respect the elders and to care for children. Perhaps the woman in the blue serape is testing me.

So she made the bed for the old man so he would be comfortable, and she cleaned the baby's cradle. She put water in the pot of beans so they wouldn't burn. She swept the entire cottage until it was spotless. Then she looked in the bucket, and there was the tripe the fish had stolen.

When she reached for the bucket a star of gold suddenly appeared on her forehead. Miranda wasn't aware of the star and returned home.

When doña Benina and her daughter Petra saw Miranda returning, they first thing they noticed was the brilliance of the star.

—Madre mía! cried Petra. What is that shining on her forehead?

Doña Benina hurried out to ask Miranda how she received the star, and Miranda told her exactly what had happened. Doña Benina knew this was a special gift, but if her daughter Petra didn't have a gold star, neither could Miranda. She took soap and water and tried to wash it off, but the more she scrubbed the brighter the star shone.

Finally she took ashes and covered the star. Then she went to her husband and told him he must butcher Petra's goat.

—But we already have enough meat, replied don Ezequiel.

—But you butchered Miranda's calf. Why not my daughter's goat? insisted doña Benina.

To keep peace in the family don Ezequiel butchered the goat. Quickly doña Benina sent her daughter to the river to wash the goat's intestines and stomach.

Petra washed the tripe and waited for the gold fish to come and steal them. When the fish didn't appear Petra threw the tripe in the river, then she went crying along the bank until she met the same woman Miranda had described.

—My daughter, why are you crying? asked the lady in blue.

—My mother sent me to wash the tripe and a fish stole them. If I don't return with them my mother will kill me.

The woman told her not to worry, and she gave Petra the same instructions she had earlier given Miranda.

Petra hurried down the river until she came to the old man's hut. She gave him a beating and threw him out of the house. She gave the baby a spanking and the threw dirt on the pot of beans. Then she went to the bucket.

When she picked up the tripe an ugly green horn appeared on her forehead. She didn't feel the horn and so she returned home.

When she was near the house Miranda saw her coming.

—Mother! Mother! she cried. Here comes Petra and she has a horn on her forehead.

—Don't lie! doña Benina answered. You're just jealous because she has a star of gold like you.

But when she stepped out the door she saw the ugly horn growing on Petra's forehead. She was horrified.

—Daughter! Daughter! What do you have on your forehead?

Petra couldn't see the horn. When she touched it she thought it was a star bigger and more beautiful that Petra's.

—I did exactly as you told me, she said. But when her mother held up a mirror Petra fainted.

Her mother tried to scrub off the horn, but couldn't. Then she tried cutting it, but the more she cut the bigger and greener and uglier it got.

—It's all your fault! doña Benina shouted at Miranda. You told us a lie!

The stepmother beat Miranda and then went to tell her husband what had happened. She insisted that don Ezequiel punish Miranda by making her the kitchen maid. She dressed the poor girl in rags and made her wash all the pots and pans.

After that they treated Miranda very badly, forcing her to do all the work in the kitchen. Each day she had to clean the fireplace, and as the days went by she grew dark with soot.

⤝ ⤞

That same year the king's son turned eighteen, and the king decided he should be married. In order to find the most beautiful girl of the kingdom, the king invited all the rich people of the region to three days of feasting.

Don Ezequiel and his wife were invited. Doña Benina ran to the village store to buy her daughter three of the most beautiful gowns she could find.

Then she ordered Miranda to comb Petra's hair and dress her for the first day of the fiesta.

—May I go? asked Miranda.

—Of course not, replied doña Benina. Look at you. You are dressed in rags and covered with soot. No one would pay attention to you.

Don Ezequiel was sorry his daughter couldn't go, but he dared not make his wife angry. That morning he had found a little spotted dog by the river, and he gave it to Miranda to keep her company.

In the evening they went to the fiesta, leaving Miranda to finish the day's chores. When she was done she sat with her dog by the fireplace and cried.

—Don't cry, the dog said. You are about to get a visitor.

As he said this, the woman Miranda had met by the river appeared.

—Why are you crying? she asked.

—My stepmother keeps me in rags. She tells me I am ugly. I work hard, but I'm not allowed to go to the king's fiesta.

—We'll do something about that, the woman said. Go to the barn and bring me three mice and a pumpkin.

When Miranda returned with the mice and pumpkin the woman splashed a magical water on her. Instantly Miranda was dressed in a lovely white gown fringed with silver. The woman placed a crown of flowers on Miranda's head to hide the star of gold.

But the most miraculous gift was a pair of perfectly shaped gold slippers for Miranda's feet.

When Miranda was ready the woman splashed the water on the pumpkin and it turned into a coach fit for a queen. Two of the mice turned into handsome white horses and the other became a coachman.

—Now you can go to the king's fiesta, the woman said. But you must return before midnight or something terrible will happen.

Miranda arrived in great style at the king's palace. When she entered the hall everyone turned to admire her. She was clearly the most beautiful young woman there, but no one knew who she was. The prince was so taken by her beauty he danced only with her.

In a corner, Petra and her mother seethed with jealousy.

As the clock was about to strike midnight Miranda raced out of the hall into the coach and was driven back home. When she arrived the woman splashed water on her. Miranda was once again a ragged, soot-covered kitchen maid. The three mice scurried away and the pumpkin lay by the door.

The following day was the second day of the king's fiesta, and again Miranda had to dress her sister for the ball. While Miranda was combing her hair Petra told her about the princess who had appeared at the dance. The prince had run after her, but she had disappeared.

—I hope she doesn't come tonight, said Petra. I intend to marry the prince.

They went off, leaving Miranda with her little dog. Shortly thereafter the woman appeared and helped Miranda dress in a rose silk gown with silver fringe, and the same gold slippers.

The moment she entered the hall the prince went to her side. He introduced her to his parents and she sat with them. All the guests wondered who she was. But as midnight approached Miranda ran out and rode her coach back home.

Shortly thereafter her parents and Petra returned. The women were fuming because the prince had paid attention only to the young woman nobody knew.

The third and last night of the king's fiesta arrived. Petra and her mother locked Miranda in the kitchen and hurried off to the dance.

Miranda and her little dog weren't alone for long. The woman appeared with a blue gown with silver fringe and the gold slippers. Miranda looked more beautiful than ever as she mounted the fine coach.

—Be back by midnight, the woman warned her.

Upon seeing her, the prince immediately went to her. Everyone wanted to know who she was, but she revealed nothing. The prince danced with her all night.

Miranda forgot the time until she saw her gown begin to change into rags. She bolted out of the dance hall for her coach, losing one of her gold slippers as she ran out the door.

The coach had changed into a burro. She mounted the animal and rode away, losing the second slipper on the road.

The prince ran after her, but he found only the gold slipper, which he put in his pocket.

That night on the road home Miranda's parents found the second slipper and took it with them.

A few days later the prince announced that he was looking for the young woman who had lost the gold slipper. If the shoe fit, he would marry her.

First he tried the shoe on all the rich young women of the realm, but the slipper fit none. Then the prince went from house to house until he came to don Ezequiel's home.

Doña Benina ran out to greet the prince and his servants.

—The shoe belongs to my daughter, she said. See, we have the matching slipper. She is the girl you're looking for. There is no need for her to try on the slipper.

The prince looked at Petra's green horn and shivered. He was sorry he had given his word to marry. He turned to look at Miranda, but since she was dressed in rags he didn't recognize her.

—Should we try the slipper on her? he asked.

—Of course not, replied doña Benina. She's just the cleaning girl.

With this she grabbed Miranda and threw her into the kitchen. But the prince wasn't satisfied. Perhaps he had seen something in Miranda's eyes.

—Take my daughter and marry her, doña Benina insisted.

—Not today, said the prince. I'll come back tomorrow with my parents.

The next day the king and the queen, and the prince, and all their retinue returned in a grand coach. Doña Benina had dressed Petra in a fine silk dress, and she hid Miranda under the large tub used for kneading dough.

—We have come for the young woman who owns the slipper, said the king.

—That's me, said a smiling Petra. See, I own the other slipper.

She climbed into the coach. But the prince was still unhappy. They were about to leave when the little dog by the door began to growl.

—Miranda is hidden under the tub, he seemed to say.

One of the servants understood the dog. He called the prince and together they followed the dog to the tub.

They lifted the tub and found Miranda. He asked her to try on the slipper, and the fit was perfect.

—You are the princess who came to the dance, he said, surprised and pleased.

He turned and told his servants to get Petra and her mother down from the coach. Doña Benina was very angry.

—You're making a mistake, she told the king and queen. Can't you see this ragged, dirty girl is only a maid!

She pulled Miranda away from the prince, took off the gold slippers, and threw her in the kitchen. Then she tried unsuccessfully to squeeze Petra's feet into the slippers.

Inside the kitchen the lady in the blue serape appeared to Miranda.

—Maybe if we dress you up like a princess they will believe you, she said smiling.

She took the plain straw broom and turned it into a comb which she used to comb Miranda's hair. As she did so, Miranda's rags turned into a beautiful blue gown.

—Now I know who you are, she told the woman. You are the Virgin Mary and you have answered my prayers. How can I ever thank you?

—You did so by not beating the old man in the hut. He is St. Joseph. And the baby is my son Jesus. The house you cleaned is their church. You are a good daughter. Now go and receive your just reward.

Miranda stepped outside, and her beauty shone so bright it dazzled those who turned to see her.

—You are the princess I have sought, said the prince. He took the gold slippers and placed them on her feet. Will you marry me? he asked.

—Yes, Miranda replied. But I must take my father with me.

Poor don Ezequiel was more than happy to get away from doña Benina and her daughter.

So all rode to the castle where the prince and Miranda were married. The wedding feast lasted for days, and Miranda and the prince lived very happy together.

As for the envious doña Benina and her daughter, no one knows what happened to them. Some say she is still trying to cut the ugly green horn off her daughter's forehead.

he Governor felt very relaxed when Serafina finished her story. Her soothing voice lent a special quality to the fairy tale. He remembered his mother telling him a version of the story.

"I heard that story as a child," he said, looking at Serafina. "The bad stepmother punishes the beautiful stepdaughter. It brought back a memory. My mother, may her soul rest in peace, used to tell me stories. Perhaps that's where I acquired my passion for the old cuentos, and the romances that are so popular today."

He had to give the young woman credit. She could spin a story the way a spider spins a well-crafted web. As she told the story he was caught in its silky threads, captive to her voice and the rise and fall of her breath as she slowed the story then quickened it. He felt Miranda's sadness, then her joy.

"You are an excellent storyteller," he said. "But it's late. You should be in bed."

He rose, walked to the door, and called Gaspar.

"Yes, Your Excellency."

"Thank you for staying up late, Gaspar. It is time for the girl to retire." The Governor turned to Serafina. "Good night. Thank you for sharing your gift of stories."

"Good night, Your Excellency," she replied and followed Gaspar out of the room.

The Governor warmed his hands at the fireplace. The glowing embers cast a soft light in the room.

I have lost the bet again, he thought. But to hear Serafina's stories was worth it. Too tired to make his way to his bedroom he lay on the sheepskin rug in front of the fireplace and covered himself with his coat.

In a moment he was asleep, dreaming he saw himself as the young prince riding in a coach with Serafina. It was spring, and the apple blossoms filled the air with a sweet fragrance. The dream was so pleasant he felt giddy with happiness.

He sat up and heard a rooster crowing, greeting the dawn. The room was cold. What did the dream mean? He got up quickly and threw wood on last night's coals.

Is she the daughter I never had? The thought startled him. Serafina was a Pueblo Indian, and he was Spanish. But it was not so far-fetched. Some of the women of the villa took Indian girls and raised them as their own.

He opened the door and shouted for the guard. "Gaspar!"

"Yes, Your Excellency?" replied the rumpled guard, jumping up from the chair where he had spent the night.

"The girl?"

"All is well, Your Excellency, I delivered her to jail as you commanded."

"Jail? But how stupid of me! The jail has little protection from the cold, and she's in there with the other prisoners. No, this won't do. How could I be so insensitive?"

"What would you have me do, Your Excellency?" asked Gaspar.

"You? Why, there's nothing you can do. This is a task for doña Ofelia. You? You can have don Alfonso assemble the prisoners. Everything should be ready in one hour."

"Yes, Excellency," Gaspar saluted, and went off to do the Governor's bidding.

The Governor hurried to bathe, eat breakfast, and meet the day dawning over the Sierra Madre.

"Doña Ofelia," said the Governor to the cook, "I have been negligent with the girl. The prisoner. She should not be in the stockade, in the cold. Can you prepare a room for her?"

"Yes, Your Excellency. There's a spare room on the east side, my sewing room. It has a fireplace, I can put in a bed and a table and give her my sewing basket so she will have something to do."

"Excellent!" The Governor smiled. "She is, after all, a young woman. She needs the privacy."

"Still," the old woman said, pausing to pour coffee for the Governor. "Some will talk . . ."

"Because I am moving the girl into my residence? It's the proper thing to do. Let them talk. My enemies would spread gossip if I killed a fly."

"Yes, that is true," doña Ofelia replied.

The Governor rose from his breakfast and walked out to greet a bright and clear day. A large crowd was already gathered around the prisoners. Some had come from as far as Galisteo. By now the word was spreading up and down the Río Grande: the Governor had pardoned one of the Indian rebels. What would he do with the rest?

The Governor emerged from his residence and greeted his maese de campo, his captains, and don Alfonso. Then he looked at the prisoners, his gaze finding Serafina. She wore a plain buffalo robe over her buckskin dress, but even dressed so simply, she looked like a princess.

The white gown? he thought. But of course, it's only for storytelling. By day she considers herself just another prisoner.

"Let us proceed, gentleman," said the Governor, taking a seat at the small table where don Alfonso had spread his papers, inkwell, and quill pens.

"Shall I commence by reading the indictment?" asked don Alfonso.

"Yes," replied the Governor. "Every detail should be recorded in these sensitive matters. Let the man state his name and pueblo."

Capitán Márquez nodded and the Indian first in line stepped forward. He was a stocky man. Wrinkles ran along his hard, brown face.

"Me llamo Pablo Cantú," he said in Spanish. "I am a Cochiti Pueblo man."

Ah, some in the crowd nodded. Cochiti Pueblo had not taken easily to Spanish rule. The Cochiti people remained rebellious. Surely the Governor would punish this man.

"How plead you?" asked don Alfonso.

"I am guilty," replied the man.

A loud murmur rose from the crowd. Had they heard correctly? The man was pleading guilty.

"Guilty," repeated the Governor. "Do you understand what you're saying?"

"Yes, I understand. I am guilty of taking care of my family and my pueblo. I joined my vecinos to talk, as I always do. In our conversation we would decide what to do when your soldiers come to take our corn and blankets. We did not plan to make war. We planned to come and speak to the Governor. If you make me a slave my family will go hungry this winter. If you send me away from my land I will never plant corn again. I will die in a foreign land. To die in a foreign land means I will never see my ancestors again."

A hush fell over the crowd. The man had spoken with sincerity. The winter had been hard, and a large percentage of the corn crop had withered under the drought of summer. Spaniards and Indians alike were surviving on the most meager stores.

The Governor cleared his throat. He looked at Serafina. Her eyes said the man spoke the truth.

"What say you, Capitán Márquez?"

The captain stepped forward. "As I stated yesterday, according to our informant this man met with the others to plot rebellion."

"But who is this informant?" interjected the Governor. "Did you find weapons?"

"No, Your Excellency."

"And did this man or his neighbors resist?"

"No, Your Excellency."

At that moment a man stepped forward from the crowd. He was a short stocky Spaniard, a farmer with a bulbous nose and a thick mustache.

"If you will allow me to speak," he said hesitantly.

The Governor nodded. "State your name and purpose."

"Me llamo Fernando Chávez. I am a farmer in the Valle de Atrisco. As you know some of us have moved south of Bernalillo to the farms of doña Luisa. We farm there in the Alameda."

The crowd drew forward. What did this man have to reveal about the trial in progress? All leaned forward to listen.

"Go on, señor," said the Governor. "Speak up."

"I know this man Pablo Cantú. When my family moved to Atrisco, our cart broke down on la Bajada. This man from Cochiti helped us. He lent me corn seed for planting. He showed me the best land to farm. That winter he brought me a deer he had killed. It saved my family from starvation. I think he is a good man. That is all I have to say."

Many in the audience nodded. They all knew Indian families who had helped them. The Españoles and the native farmers got along quite well, helping each other.

All the missions along the Río Grande cultivated corn and vegetables, fruit trees and vineyards. In the spring the Spaniards and natives gathered to clean the acequias, the irrigation ditches that fed river water into the fields. Some Españoles had learned the Pueblo languages: Tiwa, Tewa, Towa, and Keres. A few had even learned Zuni. The Indians had learned Spanish, to communicate with the Spaniards and to use as a common language amongst themselves.

Farming and the care of sheep led to commonalities as the Spaniards and Indians learned from each other. It also led to dissension as the Spaniards encroached on Indian lands. Most of the disputes were settled amicably; some smouldered with deep resentment.

Perhaps the deepest conflict was created by the friars who tried to force the Indians to give up their religion. The Franciscan friars insisted that the Indians follow only the Catholic religion. They worked hard at stamping out the Kachina dances of the Pueblos.

The Indians were forced to build mission churches in their pueblos, to be baptized, and to accept the Catholic religion. This the Pueblo Indians did, but they also insisted on keeping their own ways. This conflict between the friars and the Indians was a burning issue.

"Thank you," said the Governor, clearing his throat. "It seems the evidence in support of Pablo Cantú is weightier than that against him. As Governor of New Mexico, I move to dismiss the charges against this man."

A murmur went up from the crowd. Some smiled, some frowned. The captains glanced nervously at each other.

"Yes," continued the Governor. "Free the man. He has been a good neighbor, as señor Chávez has testified. In the face of the little evidence against him, it is better to be merciful and err on the side of forgiveness than to imprison a just man."

The Governor looked at Serafina and smiled.

"Give the prisoner food and have him return home. Tomorrow is another day, and one more prisoner will be tried. In the meantime, the day is warm. There is much work to be done."

And tonight, the Governor thought, I will ask Serafina to tell me one of her stories. What more could a man want than a daughter sitting at his side reciting the cuentos he loves?

The remaining prisoners were led back to the stockade, except for Serafina. Doña Ofelia pulled her aside and whispered to her that from now on she would have her own room in the Governor's residence.

The crowd dispersed. It was a beautiful day in la Villa de Santa Fé. Warm enough to air out homes, cut wood, repair harnesses, hunt, perhaps just meet along the southern exposure of the adobe walls and visit with neighbors. There in la resolana a man found relief from aching bones.

There would be plenty of visiting, and the mitote and arguments would all be on one topic: Why had the Governor released two prisoners?

Doña Ofelia knew the girl was a storyteller. And Gaspar also knew. Two nights in a row he had listened outside the Governor's office. He, too, was enthralled by her stories. And he was not surprised when after dinner the Governor sent him to bring Serafina to his office.

The young guard did as he was told. He led the girl through a dark, narrow hall to the Governor's office. He then sat near the door to listen. Through the cracks in the wood door he heard the Governor greet Serafina.

"Do you want to hear another story?" asked Serafina. "At the same price?"

"Absolutely," replied the Governor.

And so Serafina began the story of Pedro de Ordimalas.

SIX

The Adventures of Pedro de Ordimalas

There is a village in New Mexico which is very well known for its picaros, rascals who love to play tricks on people. I will not name the town, but its reputation is well known. Perhaps you have heard of the place.

In this village lived a widow and her two sons, Juan and Pedro. They were called Manito Juan and Manito Pedro by the paisanos. Juan was a well-behaved boy who tried to help his mother by taking care of goats, but Pedro was a rascal. People said Pedro was slow-witted, but he was really a trickster at heart. Getting the best of people was his greatest talent.

One day as Juan was going off to tend the goats, he instructed Pedro to be sure to feed their invalid mother. Pedro cooked shaquegue, a thin gruel made from toasted wheat flour. The family was so poor this is all they had to eat.

When the gruel was ready Pedro forced it down his mother's throat so fast that she choked and died.

—Que carajo! he exclaimed. I've killed my mother. But I won't take the blame.

He washed her face, combed her hair, and dressed her in her Sunday clothes. Then he sat her on a chair and placed her in front of the door. When Juan came home and pushed the door open, it toppled the chair and the old lady fell to the floor.

—Look what you've done! cried Pedro. You've killed our mother!

—Oh, dear mother, what am I going to do without you, Juan began to cry. What shall we do?

—Bury her, replied Pedro.

—But we have no money to pay for a funeral.

—I will give her a grand funeral, said Pedro.

—But how? asked his brother.

Pedro took the body outside and tied it on top of the burro. Then he led the animal to the priest's wheat field and let it loose. When the workers saw the burro eating the wheat they threw stones at it. The burro bolted and the body fell off.

Pedro went to complain to the priest.

—Look what your workers have done. They killed my mother.

—Dear Lord! cried the worried priest. If you forgive me I'll give her a grand mass, a big funeral, and I'll give you a hundred gold pieces.

Pedro was satisfied. They buried his mother and he left home to see the world. When he came to a huge tree he scattered a few coins around the tree. Then he sat to wait.

Two merchants came by and saw Pedro gathering the coins.

—What is this? one asked.

—A money tree, replied Pedro. Coins fall from it all day long. But I will sell it for fifty pesos.

The merchants paid Pedro and sat down to wait for coins to fall. Pedro pocketed the fifty gold coins and went off whistling.

When the merchants saw they had been tricked they sent their workers to catch Pedro and drown him. The workers caught Pedro, tied him in a sack, and went off to find a deep spot in the river. While they were gone a shepherd came by and saw that there was a body in the sack.

—Why are you in the sack? he asked Pedro.

—My family wants to marry me to a beautiful princess, but I refuse, explained Pedro. But if you want to marry her, get me out of the sack and climb in.

—Gladly, said the shepherd. He freed Pedro and got into the sack. When the workers returned they threw the shepherd in the river and drowned him.

For a time Pedro worked for a rich man who instructed him to clean the wheat field. Pedro burned it to the ground, the wind blew away the ashes, and the field was clean.

The man was so angry he told Pedro not to do any more farmwork. Instead, Pedro was assigned to take care of the man's son.

When the boy misbehaved, Pedro beat him with a stick. The boy quickly learned manners, but the boy's mother begged the father to get rid of Pedro.

Then Pedro returned home and married Repunosa. They had children, but Pedro wouldn't settle down. He spent his time at the gambling house in the village, playing cards.

One day Jesus and St. Peter came by the gaming place to see who would offer charity. The gamblers gave nothing. In fact, they ran Jesus and St. Peter out of the house.

Pedro was broke, but he borrowed fifty cents from his gambling friends. Then he ran after Jesus and St. Peter and gave them the coins.

—You are the only man to give us charity, said Jesus. For that I will reward you. Ask for a gift and it shall be yours.

—I only want my fifty cents back, replied Pedro.

—That is not enough, insisted Jesus, ask for more.

—I would like to be able to go to a place and if I don't want to leave, not even God can make me leave.

Jesus found this a strange request, but he granted it.

—Ask for more, he said.

—I want a deck of cards so I can win every time I play.

—Granted. Ask for more.

—I want a little drum. Whoever plays it cannot get away from it until I release them.

—Very well, said Jesus. Ask for more.

—My brother, my wife and children suffer very much. Take them to heaven.

—But they have to die before I can take them to heaven, said Jesus.

—That's all right, Pedro said.

—I will do as you say. What else do you want?

—When it is my turn to die, take me as I am to heaven.

Jesus shook his head. Pedro had finally asked for too much. But he had to keep his promise.

—Very well, your wishes are granted.

Jesus and St. Peter went on down the road to Santa Fé, and Pedro returned to the gambling house.

He played with his new deck and won every time. He became addicted to the game and didn't even go home to eat.

When the neighbors came to tell him his family was dead, Pedro returned and buried them. Now he had all the money he wanted and no one to share it with. For a while he was very happy.

One night he was sleeping in front of his fireplace when he heard a knock at the door. When Pedro opened the door he saw la Muerte, death.

—Who are you? asked a frightened Pedro.

—I am Death Who Rides a Skeleton Horse. Señor Jesucristo has sent me for you.

—Very well, agreed Pedro. But first grant me a small request. Sit at the drum and beat it. My neighbors will hear it and come. I will give my fortune away to the poor people before I die.

Death sat at the drum and beat it. When she began to beat it she discovered she couldn't leave the drum.

Pedro went to sleep, got up the next morning, ate, and left for the gambling house, leaving Death a prisoner at the drum.

Eight days later Pedro returned. A very hungry and frustrated Death still sat at the drum.

—Pedro, you must free me! Señor Jesucristo is waiting for me!

—I'll let you go if you add twenty years to my life.

—Very well, agreed Death, and Pedro let her go. She mounted her skeleton horse and went to report what had happened.

Jesus got angry. He sent Death Who Carries an Ax to take care of Pedro. He was eating breakfast when Death knocked on the door.

—Have you come for me, my comadre?

—Yes. Jesucristo sent me for you.

—I'm ready, said Pedro. But first let me call the poor people so I can give them my money. Señor Jesucristo has given me a lot, and I wish to share it. Please sit and play the drum so they will come.

Death sat to play the drum and could not move. Pedro went off to gamble, returning eight days later.

—Turn me loose! Death cried angrily.

—I will if you take away the years the first death gave me and add a new lifetime.

—Very well, Death agreed, and left in a haste to report to Jesus.

Jesus grew very irritated. Pedro's time on earth had ended, but he wasn't cooperating. He decided to send his most powerful Death, doña Sebastiana, the Skeleton Death That Rides on a Cart. Pedro could not escape her deadly arrows.

Pedro was making shaquegue for breakfast when doña Sebastiana arrived in her creaking cart.

—Buenos días, comadre, Pedro greeted death.

—Buenos días, Pedro. El Señor Jesucristo has sent me for you. He has a job for you.

—And what is that?

—He wants you to go to Limbo to take care of the little angels.

Pedro knew that babies who died before they were baptized went to Limbo. Well, he wasn't about to go take care of babies.

—I will, he said. But first will you play my drum?

It was too late. Doña Sebastiana had strung an arrow into her bow. The instant the arrow pierced Pedro he closed his eyes. When he opened them he found himself in Limbo, surrounded by the souls of beautiful babies.

—So, you weren't baptized, said Pedro. I can fix that.

He dipped the babies in a fountain of water, but he held them there so long he almost drowned them.

Soon the babies went to complain to Jesus that Pedro was drowning them.

—Please get rid of him, they begged.

Jesus called Pedro.

—Ay, Pedro, even the innocent babes of Limbo can't stand you.

—I was only baptizing them, Pedro explained.

—I am going to send you to Purgatory.

So Pedro went to Purgatory, where souls had to spend some time doing penance before they were admitted into heaven.

—I can help you do your penance faster, Pedro said to the poor souls.

He made a whip and began to whip every soul in sight. One soul escaped and went to complain to St. Peter.

—Please tell Jesus that Pedro is tormenting us.

St. Peter took the complaint to Jesus. By this time Jesus was very frustrated with Pedro.

—Send him to hell, He said. Maybe the devils can put up with him.

So they sent Pedro to hell, where the devils were getting ready to have a feast. They needed plenty of fuel for the fires, so they sent Pedro to bring firewood. With each load of wood Pedro also collected trementina, pine sap.

Pedro had to set the tables and chairs for the feast, and he put the pine sap on each chair. When the devils were through eating they told Pedro to clear the table.

—I can't clear the table until we sing "Bendito." It is our custom to thank the Lord for our food.

—No, don't sing it! the Chief Devil shouted. In hell they couldn't stand to hear the name of the Lord. But Pedro sang anyway.

—Bendito, bendito, bendito sea Dios! Bendito y alabado y ave María Purísima! he cried for all to hear.

The devils were outraged. Their ears hurt to hear the holy names. They jumped up, but the chairs stuck to them. In the uproar they bumped into each other. Pedro had locked the doors to hell, so they couldn't escape.

He shouted louder.

—Ave María Purísima!

One of the devils finally jumped out a window and went to tell St. Peter they couldn't stand Pedro in hell. St. Peter took the complaint to Jesus.

—Bring him to me, said Jesus. When Pedro stood before him Jesus said, What am I going to do with you?

—Let me go to heaven, replied Pedro.

Jesus shook his head. He knew Pedro would drive the angels crazy.

—I can't let you in heaven, but you can go to a meadow nearby and take care of a flock that belongs to St. Peter.

So Pedro went to take care of the sheep. In the distance he spied a beautiful city surrounded by a great wall which he tried to scale but couldn't. Finally he found a huge gate that led into the city, but St. Peter was guarding it.

—What place is this? asked Pedro.

—This is heaven.

—Let me in.

—I cannot, replied St. Peter.

—At least let me peek in to see what it looks like.

St. Peter thought that couldn't hurt anything, so he opened the door so Pedro could see heaven. St. Peter didn't know his namesake very well. The minute he opened the door Pedro slipped in.

—Get out! St. Peter ordered him.

—I won't, replied Pedro. I like it here.

A worried St. Peter went to tell Jesus what had happened.

—Pedro! Jesus shouted, clearly frustrated by the rascal. Get out. You don't belong here.

—Señor, I won't get out. Don't you remember you promised that if I went to a place and didn't want to leave, not even God could make me?

—Yes, I remember my promise. But I didn't say in what form you could remain. I am going to make you a rock.

—Very well, Pedro agreed. But please make me a rock with eyes so I can see the angels everyday.

So the Lord made Pedro a rock so he couldn't get into trouble. But he gave him eyes so he could enjoy the beauty of heaven. And there he sits today, a rascal who through his craftiness connived his way into heaven.

SEVEN

The flames in the fireplace and the candles on the table cast playful shadows on the walls. The Governor smiled and nodded. He had heard the stories of Pedro de Ordimalas. The man was a rascal, a *picaro* in the Spanish tradition. But he was also crafty like Odysseus, the hero of the Greek epic poem. Pedro thought ahead and laid out his plans.

And the Kingdom of New Mexico was like the world of Odysseus: survival was everything. The Spanish colonists had brought Pedro's stories with them, and they were popular because even under the worst of circumstances, Pedro laughed and kept hope alive.

"Excellent," the Governor whispered. "You have taken several of Pedro's adventures and stitched them together like a tapestry. You are a true weaver of tales, and to keep my promise I will release tomorrow's prisoner."

"Thank you, Your Excellency," replied Serafina, rising. "That is my only desire."

What a wonderful young woman she is, thought the Governor. Her only desire is the freedom of her compatriots. The thought of a daughter stirred again in the Governor's heart. Someone he could care for, someone with whom to share his ideas, his books, his love of horses. And later, when his term was done, someone to return with him to Spain.

The Governor sighed. Ah, these silly thoughts. Serafina and I are too far apart in nature and circumstances. She is a native, and I am the Governor. I have my duty to my people, and she to hers.

"Will there ever come a time when we can live in peace?" he asked.

He thought of withdrawing the question. After all, the Governor should not ask a young Indian woman her opinion. But he felt he could trust her.

"Perhaps," she replied. "After all, each one of your villages was settled next to one of our pueblos. After so many years of living side by side a few of the Españoles have taken wives from the pueblos. They are not married in the church, but they have children. They plant, irrigate, and harvest as we do. We go to church to honor la Virgen and Jesucristo. Some of your people attend our dances at the pueblos."

"True." The Governor nodded. "And yet plots against us, the Castillos as your people call us, keep boiling up."

"Perhaps we remember the history of the first governor, don Juan de Oñate," Serafina said, "and what he did to the men of Acoma. Don Juan was a conquerer, and so we live as a conquered people. In our tradition we keep history alive. Our stories tell of the battles we have fought against the Castillos. The Battle of Acoma is one of the most painful. The governor's cruelty will never be forgotten. It will haunt your people for many generations."

"But the English and the French have also practiced cutting off the feet of runaway slaves," said the Governor. "It's a practice of the colonial to intimidate the native."

"A practice to keep us enslaved," answered Serafina.

"Am I right in freeing the prisoners? Will my decisions be seen as a sign of goodwill?" he asked.

"Yes," she replied. "Still, your priests continue to forbid us the practice of our religion. They destroy the kivas and the sacred objects. They do not allow the Kachina dances."

"Ah, yes," the Governor said. "The Franciscans are a thorn even in my side."

He knew it was a question of power, a struggle between the civil and ecclesiastical authorities. The Franciscans wanted to control the lives of the Pueblo Indians. The wanted the entire tierra adentro of New Mexico to be a mission for conversion. The Spanish governors insisted they were in charge. This contention for power tore at the social fabric, affecting the lives of everyone.

The Governor sighed. He didn't want the mood of the story to dissipate. He was thankful for Serafina's gift of storytelling. Still, her opinions were well founded, and they disturbed him.

"Thank you for the story. You may go now," he said abruptly.

Surprised, Serafina raised an eyebrow. Ah, the Governor likes to listen to the cuentos but not to the suffering of my people. Very well. He has his role to play, and I have mine.

She walked to the door and stepped outside. An eager Gaspar was waiting to escort her back to her cell.

"I heard your story," he whispered as they walked through the narrow chambers of the residence. The candle he held cast just enough light for them to see a few feet ahead.

Serafina paused. She knew the young guard listened outside the door, but until tonight he had never spoken to her.

"Please don't tell the Governor," he blurted. "I can't help myself. I know the stories you tell."

Serafina nodded.

"Everyone knows the cuentos. My parents recite the stories. But the way you tell them is enchanting."

"What is your name?"

"Gaspar García, a sus ordenes." He was so overcome with Serafina's presence that he almost saluted. When he extended his arm he almost dropped the candle.

"Careful," Serafina said, steadying his hand. "Sit," she said, pointing to the wood banco in the hallway. They sat.

"Thank you," he stuttered. He felt awkward sitting beside her, but grateful for her attention.

"So you know Pedro's stories?"

"Yes."

"He is a trickster."

"I don't understand."

"You call him a picaro, we call him a trickster. We have many stories about tricksters. Like Coyote. He's always getting in trouble, but his foibles teach us something about ourselves or nature."

Gaspar nodded. "Perhaps Pedro de Ordimalas teaches us that people are crafty. Instead of dealing directly with each other we spend more time plotting how to get the best of others. We even try to foil death."

"Not even a picaro can cheat death."

"No one can cheat death."

"Maybe the storyteller can," Serafina said in a conspiratorial voice.

Gaspar was puzzled for a moment. "Ah, yes, your stories cheat death. The Governor agreed to release a prisoner for each story he enjoys. But the prisoners were not sentenced to death."

"They were to be sentenced to slavery in Nueva España, to the mines in Durango. To our people it is death to be separated from our families and the earth of our pueblos."

"I see . . ."

"The story cheats death in another way," Serafina continued. "You see, the stories will live long after we are gone and forgotten."

"Yes," Gaspar replied.

He looked into Serafina's face and couldn't believe how lucky he was to be sitting next to her. Something about her presence made him feel comfortable. He could talk freely with her. He did not know any other young women in Santa Fé who were as easy to talk to.

"Where do you live, Gaspar?"

"Here in the villa."

"With your parents?"

"Yes."

"What do they say of the Governor's release of the prisoners?"

"They say it is an act of charity. My father owns a herd of sheep. He knows how hard the Indians—your people—work. He doesn't agree with the way we treat your people."

"It is difficult for us," said Serafina. "When the first governor of the Españoles came he brought new laws. One such law is called encomienda, and so my parents, and every neighbor, must pay tribute. We pay in corn and blankets, and when winter comes we go hungry and freeze."

"But the encomendero protects you from the Apaches," Gaspar said.

Serafina frowned. "What about repartimiento, which forces us to work the fields of your people, to build missions—"

"But you get paid for your labor, fed, and protected. And if you are mistreated, by law you have the right to report the man who hires you."

Serafina sighed. "True, the laws of the Council of the Indies protect us, but the laws on the books are not always followed to the letter."

"Yes, I know," Gaspar agreed.

Serafina knew there were others like the young man Gaspar who were sympathetic to the Indians.

"It is difficult for two different cultures to live together," Serafina said.

"Maybe it would be easier if men didn't desire power," Gaspar answered. "The authorities feel they must control the Indians or there will be an uprising. I love this land. But the way it is now, there is too much conflict. I want to change that."

"Before it's too late," said Serafina.

"Perhaps together we can find answers."

"Perhaps," she agreed and rose. "Now I must return to my room."

Gaspar led her to the small room and said goodnight.

~⟨ ⟩~

The following morning the Governor rose early, ate a hearty breakfast, then ordered that his steed be saddled. He rode hard into the hills east of the villa. He rode until he arrived at the crest of a hill of the piedmont. Here he dismounted and let his well-lathered horse rest. He, too, was sweating from the ride.

He stood and looked down on the villa. The Governor's residence, offices, the jail, a chapel, and an arsenal were built in contiguous fashion around the perimeter of the plaza. These casas reales included the four sentry towers, two on the north side and two on the south. An impenetrable fortified compound, thought the Governor. Not a stone castle of Spain, but a castle of adobe.

The mud homes of the villagers spread mostly south of the central plaza. There were six vecindades, districts where the people lived. Near each home lay the fallow fields that in the summer were irrigated by the acequia madre fed by the river. Yes, La Villa de Santa Fé de los Españoles had grown since it was founded by then Governor Peralta in 1610.

The homes on the north side of the plaza also had their vegetable gardens, vineyards, and olive groves.

"They would not understand the life we endure here in the court of Spain," he said aloud. "Not even in Mexico City, the capital of New Spain."

This was the northernmost frontier of Nueva España, the northern antipodes as far as Spain was concerned. Rough, uncivilized, a frontier like no other.

We must depend on ourselves, he thought. Depend on our neighbors. This is the land of legend, Cíbola. The land the Aztecs of Mexico called Aztlán, their homeland. Now it is ours, for better or for worse.

Ours, all of us, español, indio, criollo, mestizo, castizo, mulatto, chino, lobo, gibaro, zambo or whatever we call ourselves. We must become one people. La raza de la Nueva México.

I do not wish to return to Spain, he thought. I will stay here. I will make this land my home.

Excited by the revelation he looked over the villa, clothed with the light of dawn as the sun rose over the sierra. A new Jerusalem not only for the Sephardics amongst us, but for all of us. A shining Mecca for those of Arabic ancestry. Santa Fé! The capital of the New Continent!

"Sí se puede!" he shouted, mounting his horse, which swirled and reared up, pawing the air, whinnying as if it felt the excitement of its rider.

By the time the Governor rode into the plaza, Capitán Márquez had the prisoners lined up and ready to be tried. A buzzing, inquisitive crowd waited for the proceedings to begin. All were startled by the Governor's dramatic entrance, his horse wet with sweat sliding into a perfect halt.

The Governor alighted and greeted all present.

"Buenos dias, caballeros. Forgive my late arrival. Let the trial began," he said to the secretary.

Don Alfonso took quill in hand, dipped it in the inkwell, and called the name of the prisoner.

"The man known as Alonso Catiti from the pueblo of Santo Domingo will step forward."

A stocky man of about thirty years stepped forward, and the secretary read the charges against him. Capitán Márquez then presented his defense. But the Governor paid scant attention to the words. He looked at the crowd. All eyes were on him, not on the captain's plea for mercy.

He looked at Serafina. He was startled by the strength of her gaze, an almost defiant stare. She showed no fear. Perhaps the girl has power over my mind, he thought for the first time. He had heard that the natives practiced many kinds of witchcraft. Was it his idea to treat her like a daughter? Or had she put the thought in his mind?

He tried to shake the idea away. I am an enlightened man, he thought. I don't believe in such things. Still, there was a way to test her.

"What say you, Governor?" don Alfonso asked, leaning toward the Governor.

The Governor rose. "I say we must be merciful. Free this man and send him home with food for his family. Thus I conclude these proceedings. We have other important matters at hand. The Apaches stole some sheep a few days ago. Today we ride to catch the thieves."

He called his captain and ordered an escort be ready to ride. When the horses were saddled he and ten soldiers rode out of the villa headed north. He left in his wake a very startled citizenry. Loud exclamations and arguments had erupted in the plaza. What was happening to the Governor? Would all the prisoners be freed? And how would this help to stop the rebellion that many feared was imminent?

The Governor cared not for the dissension he left behind. He and the escort rode all day, following the tracks of an Apache raiding party until they lost them, returning to the villa late in the afternoon. The soldiers were exhausted, but the Governor seemed full of energy. After writing the viceroy in México an account of the day's excursion and a dinner of venison, he sent for Serafina.

"Good evening, Your Excellency," she said as Gaspar closed the door behind her. "You look tired."

"It has been a long day, but after a good meal a good story would relax me."

He took a cigar, the kind imported from Hispañola, and lit it at the candle flame.

"The usual agreement," he said as he sat in front of the fireplace.

"Very well," she replied and began her story.

EIGHT

Fabiano and Reyes

nce there were two kingdoms whose kings and queens were very good friends. One summer a baby was born to one of the queens, and she and her husband invited the other king and queen to baptize the boy. They christened him Fabiano.

Two years later the other queen gave birth to a baby girl, and the godparents of Fabiano were invited to baptize her. They named her Reyes. The boy and girl grew up together, spending one week at one palace and the next at the other.

The two grew up loving each other like brother and sister. Fabiano was an exceedingly handsome boy, but Reyes was not considered a beauty. When they were old enough they were sent to school to begin their studies. Fabiano took very good care of Reyes, because he loved her beyond compare.

But Fabiano was vain. He began to write love letters to one of the most beautiful girls in school. He shared the letters with Reyes because he totally trusted her.

—Reyes, he said, the girl I wrote to is the fairest in our school, and I will have only a beauty like her. I'd rather be blind than be seen with an ugly girl.

Reyes did not consider herself beautiful, and although she loved Fabiano, his comments made her feel ashamed.

—Dear Fabiano, she said, you deserve a virtuous and beautiful woman. One as handsome as you.

Throughout their school years Fabiano continued to fall in love with the loveliest girls and to despise those he considered plain.

When they completed their studies they returned home, and as was their custom they continued to visit one week at one palace and the next at the other.

The parents were so happy to have Fabiano and Reyes back home they held dances and fiestas and bullfights. Fabiano and Reyes always attended these events together, and he would dance only with the loveliest girls.

When he presented his partner to Reyes he would whisper,

—Isn't she beautiful? I'd rather be blind than have an ugly woman at my side.

One week the festivities were to be held at the palace of Fabiano's father, who promised to bring the best singers and bullfighters from across the sea. Fabiano and Reyes helped with all the preparations.

The first night of the dance Fabiano met a lovely young woman whom he immediately introduced to Reyes.

—Reyes, meet my sweetheart. Isn't she beautiful? Then he whispered to her. You know I would never have an ugly woman as my girlfriend.

—Yes, replied Reyes. The woman who marries you must be beautiful and virtuous.

The following night Reyes felt so discouraged she came to the dance in a plain linen dress.

Fabiano reproached her.

—Reyes, why are you dressed in linen? A virtuous princess like you should be dressed in the finest silk.

—Oh my dear Fabiano, you know an ugly woman like me should not dress in silk. I don't deserve fine dresses; the most common will do for me.

—But I would be ashamed to present you to my sweethearts who dress in silk while you wear plain linen.

—The women you fall in love with are beautiful and deserve silk, replied Reyes. I will dress to match how I feel.

Reyes's father had invited a well-known singer from across the sea to sing, but the singer was drowned when the ship sank.

Reyes went to Fabiano and explained the situation.

—My father promised his guests that the singer would appear tonight, but now that is impossible. So that my father doesn't lose his honor, I will sing tonight.

—No, no, replied Fabiano. Singing is not for a princess. People will criticize you, and then I will be ashamed.

In spite of Fabiano's protests, Reyes decided to sing for the assembled guests. No one had ever heard her sing before, so all were surprised at her lovely, melodious voice. Even the arrogant Fabiano sat spellbound.

By the time Reyes finished her song Fabiano's heart was throbbing with love. Immediatedly he went to Reyes and asked her to dance.

—Oh, you wouldn't like to be seen dancing with an ugly woman, she replied. Please excuse me.

The festivities ended and the guests left, but Fabiano's new-found passion would not let him rest. He had fallen in love with Reyes. Quickly he went to his parents and asked them to ask for Reyes's hand in marriage.

Of course the king and queen were very happy, and, as was the custom, they went to ask permission for their son to marry Reyes.

All were shocked at Reyes's refusal.

—I cannot marry a man who despises those he calls ugly. A person should not be judged by the looks God has given. Fabiano should marry someone as beautiful as he.

When Fabiano heard Reyes's answer he grew very depressed. He couldn't get over the love he felt for Reyes. After a month he went to his friend, a captain, and asked him to intercede. The captain agreed to go to Reyes and tell her that Fabiano was very much in love with her and wished to marry her.

Reyes confessed to the captain that she had always loved Fabiano, but because he had despised ugly women so much she could not marry him.

The captain sadly reported this to Fabiano, who decided to leave his kingdom forever. He moved far away, and every other day he would write Reyes a letter expressing his love, but he never mailed them.

One afternoon while Fabiano was hunting, the rifle he was using exploded and blinded him. While he was in the hospital his father and mother died. The caretaker of their castle went to the hospital and brought Fabiano home. All the people who had once worked for the king and queen were gone; there only remained the caretaker and the old housekeeper to take care of Fabiano.

Life in the deserted castle was lonely and sad. The old housekeeper cared poorly for Fabiano.

To console himself, Fabiano took out the letters he had written Reyes, but now he could not read them.

One day his old friend the captain came to visit.

—Has Reyes come to see you? he asked.

—No, replied Fabiano. She will not see me because I spoke ill of ugly people. Without her love I am slowly dying.

The captain went to visit Reyes.

—He is alone and he is blind, he told Reyes. You and he grew up together, and yet you don't visit him. Why?

—I love Fabiano with all my heart, Reyes replied. But I believe he fell in love with my singing, not with me. Does he love me deep inside?

—Go and find out. The old housekeeper doesn't take good care of him. The food she prepares is not fit for pigs. He needs a nurse. You should be that nurse!

—Yes, Reyes agreed, I would like to take care of Fabiano. But with one condition.

—What is that?

—You must not tell him I am the nurse.

—Ah, said the captain, so that way you will discover for yourself if he loves you with all his heart.

—Yes.

—Very well, you have my word I won't tell him.

With that the captain rode off. He arrived at Fabiano's in a joyful mood.

—My dear friend, he said, I have good news. I have found a nurse who will take care of you.

—Thank you for your kindness. I only hope she can read.

The captain brought Reyes to Fabiano's castle, and when she saw the poor state he was in, she vowed to take care of him.

She heated water so Fabiano could take a bath, and she brought out his fine clothes. She prepared him good meals, and soon Fabiano regained his health. He was very happy with the nurse his friend had found.

—Nurse, he said one night, can you keep a secret?

—Yes, replied Reyes.

—You know the small suitcase I keep by my bed?

—Yes.

—Bring it to me, please.

Reyes brought the suitcase and Fabiano opened it.

—These are letters I wrote to the woman I love. Will you please read them?

Reyes began to read the letters Fabiano had written and never mailed, and as she read, tears filled her eyes. She looked at Fabiano and saw that he too was silently weeping.

The next day the captain came to visit and found Reyes in the kitchen. It was obvious she had been crying.

—Is something the matter? he asked her.

—I read Fabiano's letters last night. I know now he truly loves me.

—What are you going to do?

—I will marry him.

The captain and Reyes rode to Fabiano's castle. They found him in the garden, and at first only the captain spoke.

—My dear friend, you are alone so much. I think you should be married.

—Who would have me? asked Fabiano.

—Your nurse. She takes very good care of you.

—Yes, and I feel very close to her. But the love in my heart is only for Reyes.

—Then marry Reyes.

—She wouldn't have me when I was young, why would she have me now?

—I spoke to her, and she will marry you. You see, the nurse who has been taking care of you is Reyes herself.

Fabiano was speechless. Tears filled his eyes. Of course he had felt Reyes's presence when the nurse was near, but he did not trust his feeling.

—I would give you half my kingdom if that were true, he said with a sigh.

—It is true, said Reyes, stepping forward and taking his hand.

—I am blind and you will have me as a husband?

—I am ugly, will you have me?

—I have learned a lesson, said Fabiano. When I was young I judged people by their looks. I know now that we should love everyone equally.

—Perhaps we have both learned a lesson, said Reyes.

The two were married, and to this day they live together, taking care of each other and sharing their love.

NINE

A glint of light from the dying embers in the fireplace betrayed the Governor's tears. He turned away so Serafina might not see.

Why has the story made me sad? he thought. I am the Governor, a military man who has seen many campaigns, fought many battles. I am ruler of this miserable kingdom which I daily struggle to keep together. The Apaches now have horses and attack the Pecos, Quarai, and Abo missions, the Pueblos constantly complain, and always some of the citizens want to quit the colony and return to New Spain. The winters are bitter, the drought has lasted many years.

How can I be so affected by a story? Is it that I am like Fabiano, and I have been seeing only the ugly side of life? Are the stories really revelations of my soul? Am I Juan Oso, half man and half beast? Pedro de Ordimalas, a mere picaro pretending to be governor? Fabiano who lost the love of his life as I lost my wife?

He looked at Serafina. Can she read my heart? Is it possible she is a witch?

Yes, the thought had crossed his mind before. The Franciscan friars' chief complaint was that the Indians practiced sorcery, they prayed to pagan gods, kept masks in their kivas and held the Kachina dances.

"I'll call Gaspar," he said abruptly, rising and walking briskly to the door.

When Gaspar had led the girl away the Governor hurried out into the freezing night. A sweet scent hung over the plaza from the thin feathers of smoke that rose from villa's fireplaces.

The settlement lay embraced by night, bathed in the light of the glittering Milky Way and a pale, waxing moon. In the hills coyotes yipped, a witching cry. Higher up, where the juniper-studded hills met the mountain pine treeline, a wolf howled a long, mournful cry for its mate, and moments later she returned the call.

The sorcerers, the priests had reported, took the form of owls, coyotes, and wolves to travel about at night.

"Bah!" the Governor spat, "I am not a superstitious man."

Still, he hurried across the frozen, desolate plaza to knock on the door of the church.

Friar Tomás, his freckled face and reddish hair illuminated by the lantern he held, opened the heavy door. "Que diablo es a esta hora?"

He peered into the pale face of the Governor and for a moment couldn't recognize him.

"Ah, Your Excellency. What brings you out on such a cold night? I hope no last rites. An accident?"

"No such thing, Fray Tomás. Perhaps a case of witchcraft."

"Witchcraft!" the startled friar gasped. He peered beyond the Governor into the dark night. At night the peaceful landscape turned into the Demon's playground. No one stirred, except those men who braved the cold to drink homemade wine at the cantina of doña Patricia.

"Come in, come in," he said.

"I cannot stay," replied the Governor. "You know the girl who came with the prisoners?"

"Yes. I have attended the trial with great interest. Needless to say, your judgments have created quite a—

"Fray Tomás, that's not the matter at hand."

"Ah, yes, the girl."

"I want you to question her."

"Tonight?"

"Yes."

"This is highly unusual. I should send a message to the Custodian—"

"I don't want this request to be heard by anyone except you," interrupted the Governor. "Isn't it true that if you enter the room with the blessed Crucifix, if the woman is a witch she will cringe, cry out, and blaspheme the Holy Cross?"

"Yes, but the girl cannot be—"

"I make no accusation! I only ask that you speak to her. See how she reacts, that's all I require of you."

"Very well," a puzzled Fray Tomás replied. He disappeared for a moment and returned wearing a heavy buffalo coat, a crucifix in hand. Together they made their way back to the Governor's residence and to Serafina's room.

"Is something wrong, Your Excellency?" asked Gaspar, puzzled by the Governor's rapid exit and the appearance of the friar.

The Governor did not answer. "Knock and enter," he whispered to the friar. "Do not let her know I'm here."

The tremulous young friar made the sign of the cross, held the crucifix in front of him, and knocked.

"Enter," Serafina said, and he entered the room. Behind him the door shut tight.

Shivering, he held the cross in front of him and took hesitant steps toward Serafina.

"I come in the name of the Father, the Son, and the Holy Spirit. If there are demons in possession of your soul, I cast them out with this cross."

He stood trembling, expecting at any moment to feel the wrath of the Devil descend on him.

Instead he saw Serafina make the sign of the cross and kneel on the bare floor.

"Have you come to hear my confession, padre?" she asked.

Fray Tomás cringed. He looked down into Serafina's calm face; her dark eyes peered back at him with an innocence that mesmerized him.

"You're not a witch," he muttered.

"No, padre."

"You asked for confession . . ."

"I was raised in the mission church at my pueblo. I know all the prayers."

She closed her eyes and waited. A shudder went through Fray Tomás. He didn't know what to do. He hadn't come to confess a Christian, he had come to cast out demons. But there were no demons in the girl, only an aura that enhanced her beauty.

"Please rise, child," he managed. "Sit."

Serafina rose and sat on the cot.

"Did you come to hear my confession?" she repeated.

"No, not tonight," the confused friar answered.

For a long time the friar did not speak. Finally he asked, "Are you like the others? You believe in Christ, and yet you keep your pagan beliefs?"

"I believe in the ways of my ancestors. Christ and his mother and the saints have come to join our holy people—"

"No!" he interrupted her. "You can't believe in Christ and believe in the things of the Devil! You are not a witch, child, but it is those things of Lucifer we must drive out. Place your hands on the cross and pray with me."

He sat by her, closed his eyes, and holding the holy cross to her he began to pray. He could hear her praying, her Castilian Spanish almost as good as his.

They are all like this, he thought. We baptize them, they help us build churches, they come to mass and take the Eucharist, then they go at night to their kivas and pray to their fetishes, masks of the Devil. Why can't we drive those beliefs out of them?

He could smell the perfume of her hair, washed with soap from yucca roots. Opening his eyes he looked at her. She was only a few years younger than he, yet she was mature beyond her years.

"You're not a witch," he stammered.

"No, padre, I am not."

"You are innocent," he murmured, unsure of what to say or do. He had never dealt with a situation like this before. "Good night. I must go," he said. Outside, he was met by an anxious Governor.

"Well. What is your finding?" he asked, clutching the friar's coat.

"She's not a witch. We prayed together. She is innocent."

"I was wrong to have you question her," the Governor said, realizing he had made a mistake. "Thank you for your time, Fray Tomás . . ."

"It is nothing," the friar replied. "I shall return to pray with her," he said and disappeared into the cold night.

The Governor gathered his courage, opened the door, and entered the room. Serafina looked up at him, and after a pause she spoke.

"Why did you send the friar to question me?" she asked, her voice cold and pentrating. "I am not a witch."

"Forgive me," the Governor said. "I do not believe in witchcraft. But I had to be sure."

"Why?"

The Governor sighed. "Some of my enemies are spreading rumors; they say you have a power over me, and they attribute it to witchcraft."

"But you don't believe that."

"No, but if they can get the Inquisition to question you, they would use the trial to destroy me. I had to be sure. Now I have the friar's opinion."

"I see," Serafina said. There was discord in the villa. Those who wanted the Governor out of office would use her to accomplish their goal. The Governor had to protect himself, and her.

"I am sorry I put you through this."

"One does what one has to do," she replied.

"Believe me, I only do what I think is best for you. Now you must rest. Good night, Serafina."

"Good night, Your Excellency."

The Governor disappeared and Serafina turned to the clothes doña Ofelia had given her. She stitched late into the night, pausing only when she heard the cries of coyotes in the hills. She went to the east wall and pressed her ear against the cracks.

"Father!" she cried. The coyote cries were her father and friends camped in the hills, awaiting her release. The call was clear, a signal for her to know they were there.

Serafina blew out the candle, slipped into bed, and slept a very peaceful sleep.

The next morning the Governor ate breakfast and hurried to the trial. As before, he listened intently to the charges read against the fourth prisoner, and as the people expected, the man tried that morning was freed. The other prisoners were sent back to the stockade, and Serafina returned to her room, where she worked on the colcha she was stitching.

The Governor rode out with soldiers, still pursuing the Apaches who had raided the Picuris mission, but the raiders had disappeared.

That evening, as was by now his custom, he called for Serafina. When he saw her the concerns of the day fell away. The more he thought of her as a daughter, the more he felt free to entertain the idea. And yet the thought disturbed him, because it was something that could not be.

He greeted her cordially, offering her a chair by the fireplace.

"Do you have a story ready?" he asked kindly.

"I never have one ready," she replied. "Whatever comes to mind is the story I tell."

"You are truly gifted," he said, leaning back into his chair and closing his eyes.

TEN

The Devil's Godchild

This couple had many children. Almost all the people in the plaza where they lived were godparents to their children. When the woman gave birth to a son, the husband was ashamed to invite anyone from the plaza to baptize the baby.

—We've already asked everyone we know, he said. Today I'm going to invite the first person I meet on the road to be my son's godparent.

He went off down the road and the first person he met was the Devil. Of course the man didn't know it was the Devil, because he appeared as a caballero, riding a beautiful black horse and dressed in a suit of silk and silver buckles.

The man greeted the Devil.

—Excuse me, señor, but I'm looking for someone to baptize my new-born son, and since you're the first one I have met, I ask you to do me the honor. Will you be my compadre?

—Yes, replied the Devil, I will serve as your child's godparent—on the condition that when he is seven years old you will give him to me.

The man agreed. After all he and his wife had so many children they didn't know what to do with them all.

—I agree, said the man. When will you come to the baptism?

—I will come on Monday, the Devil answered, but we will not go to the church. Tell the minister to come to your house.

The man returned home and told his wife he had found a compadre. He didn't know the man, but it was obvious he was a real caballero.

On Monday the Devil arrived as promised, and immediately picked up the child. The Devil had filled his ears with wax so he couldn't hear the priest's prayers.

—I christen thee Pelucas, said the priest, sprinkling holy water on the baby's head.

A drop splashed on the Devil's arm and sizzled, but no one noticed.

When the baptism was done the Devil gave the parents some gold coins and promised to visit Pelucas every three months. He did this, each time bringing presents for his godchild and money for the parents.

When Pelucas was seven the Devil arrived on his black horse. By now the father was suspicious, and he tried to renege on his bargain.

—You are not a good man, said the father. I will not give my son to you.

—You cannot break a promise, replied the Devil, and struck the father dead.

He carried Pelucas away on his horse and they rode to a high, dark mountain. The devil shouted for the rocky crags to part and a deep chasm opened before them.

—Shut your eyes and don't open them till I tell you, the Devil commanded. He dug his spurs into his horse and they leapt into the abyss.

When Pelucas opened his eyes he saw a shining castle surrounded by an icy river.

—This is your home, the Devil told Pelucas. Because you can read and write, you will be my secretary. You will keep a book of every worker so he can read the history of his life and know why he came here.

When Pelucas was fifteen, the Devil decided to test him.

—I am going to walk around the world, he said. You are to take care of everything here. Take care of all my horses except the thin white one. Don't feed that horse. Here are the keys to all the rooms of the palace. You may enter every one except this one.

He pointed at a beautiful door made of gold. Then the Devil rode away to tempt sinners on the paths of the world.

Pelucas had never seen all the rooms of the palace, but now that he had the keys he visited each one. Each room contained the souls of those condemned to suffer. Each soul sat reading his history as it was written in the book of his life, but it was too late to change the evil he had done.

When Pelucas came to the room with the gold door he was curious.

—I wonder why my godfather forbids me to enter this room? Is there something he doesn't want me to see?

Pelucas opened the door and saw a glowing ball that gave off a bluish aura.

—What can this be? he wondered.

He approached the whirling fireball and held out his finger to see if it was hot. When he withdrew his finger he saw that it was encased in gold.

Enchanted by what had happened, he stuck his head into the glowing ball and it turned his hair into silky strands of gold.

—How strange, thought Pelucas. But now my godfather will know I was here. I must cover my head.

He made a wig and covered his hair. Then he ordered the workers to feed the thin white horse his godfather kept starved. Later that day when he went to visit the horse, he was surprised the horse could speak.

—You have disobeyed your godfather, said the horse. Now I must help you escape from this place. You don't know, but your godfather is the Devil. He knows what you are doing at this very moment. Hurry and bring a saddle, halter, spurs, quirt, and the comb you use to groom me.

Pelucas was shocked at this revelation, but he did as he was told. He saddled the white horse and raced out of the dark abyss he had entered years ago.

The devil has sharp ears and hears even the most quietly whispered secrets. He heard the white horse talking and hurried to his palace. Just as he suspected, Pelucas and the horse were gone. He chased after them.

Pelucas's horse sensed something following them.

—Turn and tell me what you see, it commanded.

—I see an angry whirlwind that reaches to the sky, Pelucas said.

—It is the Devil, said the horse. Throw the comb in its path.

Pelucas did as he was told and the comb became a high mountain the Devil had difficulty crossing.

After a while the horse again told Pelucas to look back.

—It's the same whirlwind, he said, and it's very close.

—Throw your quirt and spurs in its path.

Pelucas did as he was told and a big river of blood gushed out of the earth. Sharp knives and scissors flowed in the blood. When the Devil tried to swim across the river he was cut into pieces.

—Who follows us now? asked the horse.

—No one, replied Pelucas. We are safe.

—Safe for a while, said the horse. The world cannot last long without the Devil. He takes many forms and returns when you least expect him.

They went on until they came to a city where Pelucas asked the king for work.

—My orchards are dry and neglected, said the king, if you can revive them I will reward you.

Pelucas went to work, and the special gift in his gold finger allowed him to revive the fruit trees.

One very hot day he decided to take a bath in the water tanks that fed the orchard. Thinking he was alone, he took off his wig.

It was the custom of the king's daughter to stand on her balcony and watch Pelucas working. He was such a handsome fellow she had fallen in love with him. When she saw Pelucas's hair of gold she was surprised.

—This man has a very special gift, she thought, or else the hair is artificial. I must know.

She ran to her father to ask a favor.

—Father dear, she said, haven't you promised to give me whatever I desire?

—Of course I have, dear daughter. What is it you want?

—I want three hairs from the head of Pelucas.

—What a strange request, answered the king. Can't you tell Pelucas is bald? That's why he wears that ridiculous wig.

—But I want you to order him to bring me three of his actual hairs, she insisted.

—Very well, daughter, I will do so.

That afternoon when Pelucas returned from the orchards the king commanded him to bring three of his hairs. Pelucas went away very worried. He knew he had been discovered and that meant his life might be in danger.

—I am afraid, he told the white horse when he arrived home. The king has ordered me to take him three hairs from my head.

—You must do as you are told, said the white horse. One cannot disobey the king.

Pelucas took three gold hairs from his head, put them in an envelope, and delivered them to the king. The king gave the package to his daughter, who tore it open and discovered the gold hairs.

—This is an extraordinary man, she thought. I love him and must have him for my husband. She sent a maid to tell Pelucas of her love, then she hurried and told the king she wished to marry Pelucas. The king and his advisors were against it. A princess, they said, should not marry a common worker. But the princess kept insisting.

—I must get rid of this Pelucas, thought the jealous king. Then he and his counselors devised a test that would kill Pelucas.

Later, the king told his daughter he would allow her to marry Pelucas if he could pass a test. The counselors then brought Pelucas before the king.

—My queen has fled to a castle across the sea, he told Pelucas. If you can bring her and the castle to me I will let you marry my daughter.

Pelucas went away very worried. When he arrived at the stable the white horse asked him what was the matter.

—Don't worry, said the horse. Tell the king you need two large ships to carry the castle and an army to help load the castle onto the ships. Take four large pieces of meat to throw to the lions that guard the castle.

Pelucas did as he was told. He sailed three days until he came to the queen's castle. He threw the meat at the lions, got past them, and found the queen. The queen did not want to return because the king was a cruel tyrant, but she had no choice.

With great care the army of men loaded the castle onto the ships and that way Pelucas was able to deliver everything to the king.

A large crowd was waiting for them, including the king, who welcomed the queen.

—You have returned, he said to the queen. Is there anything you need?

—I dropped my keyring in the ocean, she replied. I cannot open the trunks that hold my jewels and dresses. You must go in search of it.

She is testing me, thought the king, for no one can find a keyring in the middle of the ocean. I will send Pelucas. When he returns without them I'll have him hung.

—Pelucas, my friend, you have not yet completed my order. When you returned with the queen she dropped her keyring in the middle of the ocean. You must go and find it.

Crestfallen, Pelucas returned to the stable and told his horse what the king had commanded.

—Don't worry, said the white horse, I will tell you how to perform this task. Tell the king you need the best musicians in the kingdom and a boat full of bread.

Pelucas did as he was told. Two days later he set sail. When they came to the middle of the sea they dropped anchor. Pelucas ordered the musicians to play and soon all the fish, mermaids, and mermen in the vicinity gathered to hear the music.

Then Pelucas ordered the sailors to throw bread overboard for the fish to eat. When they had eaten, one large golden fish came near the boat.

—Thank you for the music and the bread. Tell me, what can we do for you?

—I am glad you enjoyed the fiesta, answered Pelucas. I want to know if any of you have seen the keyring the queen dropped when we passed by here.

—I will ask, said the king of the fish.

They found an old, old fish who had seen the keyring. He swam down and retrieved the keys, and in this way Pelucas was able to return them to the queen.

The queen was happy, and so was the princess because now she was convinced Pelucas was a most extraordinary man.

—I will marry you, she told Pelucas.

—There is one more test he must pass, interrupted the king. Because he has delivered the queen and her castle and found the keys in the depth of the ocean, he must be a sorcerer. He must be burned alive.

The princess tried to reason with her father, but he was insistent. Pelucas went away shaking.

—I cannot escape this test, he told his white horse. I will surely die.

—What did the king say? asked the horse.

—He has ordered me to be burned alive.

—I have helped you before, I will help you again, said the horse. Here's what you must do. Tell the king to heat three large kettles. One will contain boiling lead, the other boiling lard, and the third boiling water. Next to the kettles they are to build a large fire where they intend to burn you. Nearby they must set up a tent.

Pelucas went and told the king to prepare the kettles and fires. The next morning the horse gave further instructions.

—Today you must ride me one league. Use your quirt and spurs and ride me until I am well lathered, then collect all of my sweat in a bottle. Tomorrow before you jump into the boiling kettles and fire you must cover yourself completely with my sweat.

Pelucas did as he was told. He raced the horse a league and when he returned it was sweating profusely. Pelucas gathered the sweat in a dish, then poured it into a bottle. Then he went to where a large crowd had gathered by the boiling kettles.

—I am ready for the test, he said and entered the tent where he covered himself with the horse's sweat.

When the king rang the bell Pelucas came out and jumped into the first kettle. The princess closed her eyes, but Pelucas came out alive. He jumped into the second boiling kettle and the third and finally into the huge fire at the end.

The fire was so intense Pelucas disappeared, but when the flames died down he was still alive. The firewood had burned but Pelucas hadn't even singed a finger.

The people greeted him with cheers, and they blamed the king for the horrible test he had put Pelucas through.

—You cannot do what Pelucas has done, they cried.

—Of course I can! I am the king! If Pelucas can pass the test of fire so can I.

The king walked to the large cauldron of boiling lard and jumped in. At that moment the Devil appeared.

—Hello, my friend, said the Devil to the king. You are not protected as is Pelucas. You must die.

The king died, and that afternoon the people buried him and asked Pelucas to be their king.

A great fiesta was held in the castle; the people were very happy. Even the princess, saddened as she was, attended. Pelucas spent all his time with her, and he forgot about his horse.

On the third day of the celebration Pelucas remembered his horse. He hurried to the stable and found the horse dying of thirst and hunger.

—I have neglected you, said Pelucas, hugging his horse.

—I have done all I can for you, replied the white horse, but you have abandoned me.

—It's true, replied a remorseful Pelucas. I fell in love with the princess and forgot you. But I'm here now. I will take you to the castle and take good care of you.

—It's too late, replied the horse. I am dying. It's best you put a merciful end to my life.

—No! No! I can't do that, cried Pelucas.

—I command you to kill me, the horse insisted.

With tears running down his cheeks Pelucas took a dagger and ended the horse's suffering.

As the horse died a spirit rose and spoke to Pelucas.

—Do you know who I am? the spirit asked.

—No.

—I am the spirit of your father. I was punished because I invited the Devil to baptize you. But St. Peter gave me permission to return to earth to help you. Now I say goodbye forever.

With those words the spirit disappeared.

A very sad but thankful Pelucas returned to the castle, wearing the king's crown on his head. He ruled the kingdom for many years, taking good care of the people and making the entire country prosperous.

ELEVEN

The last words of the story wrapped themselves around the thin strands of smoke that rose from the candle towards the low ceiling. There, among the latillas, the thinner aspen logs that criss-crossed the pine vigas, the smoke curled and disappeared for the night.

The story had penetrated the Governor's heart, his soul, the seat of his imagination. During the telling he had become Pelucas, passing the tests set by the tyrant king, emerging victorious from the boiling lard, lead, and water, finally walking forth from the ashes of the fire like the phoenix of ancient legends.

The story made him resolve not to burn in the crucible that was la Nueva México! He would not allow his enemies to defeat him! He would live in legend forever. He would be invincible!

But who will be my guardian spirit? he asked himself. Pelucas had his father in the form of a white horse watching over him. Who will watch over me as I face the dissident colonists, those political enemies who spread rumors about my command to the Viceroy in Mexico City? Or the friars who constantly remind me that their missionizing work is far more important than civil governance? Or the marauding Apaches? And how am I to overcome the greatest threat, those natives who plot to destroy the colony?

He opened his eyes and looked at Serafina. Was she his guardian spirit? His angel? The daughter he never had? An ally he could trust in the turbulent world of New Mexico?

"No," he whispered. Again he was placing too much trust in the girl, in her stories. They were just that, stories. He was entertained, but that was all. Looking into her dark, clear eyes he wanted to say more, to reach out and take her hands in his.

Standing, he bowed slightly. "Thank you. I enjoyed the story, but it has been a long day. I must bid you good night."

"Goodnight, Your Excellency," Serafina replied.

She exited and Gaspar led her to her room.

"I want to talk to you," he said when they reached her door. "Is it possible?"

"I see no reason why not," she said, looking into the young man's eyes and wondering what he had to say.

He was about to ask her if he could enter her room when doña Ofelia appeared, a lit taper in a candleholder in one hand and a cup of hot chocolate in the other.

"Don't just stand there," the old woman ordered, "open the door."

"A sus ordenes," replied the startled Gaspar. He opened the door and Serafina and the old woman entered. Doña Ofelia kicked the door shut behind her.

She set the cup and candle on the rough wood bench and greeted Serafina.

"Buenas noches, hijita. I brought you some hot chocolate."

"Thank you, señora, but I should not drink it."

"And why? Don't you know sweetened chocolate is a delicacy for the Españoles? Yes, they came with dreams of finding the fabled cities of Cíbola. The adventures of Cabeza de Baca filled them with fantasies. They thought they would find another Tenochtitlan here in the northern Río Bravo. Bah, dreams! Fantasies! There is no gold. But chocolate is like gold. It has to be shipped in ox-drawn carts all the way from Mexico City. It takes months to make the journey. The Aztec kings used to drink chocolate, and you refuse this cup? Why?"

"I will eat and drink only what the other prisoners eat and drink."

"Ah, I see. No, I cannot give this drink to the indios. But you need the strength, child. You are the one who frees your fellow men. Come, drink, for them. Drink to please an old woman."

Serafina smiled, took the cup, and drank. She had never tasted chocolate, and she sipped the rich drink slowly, enjoying the way it seemed to awaken every taste bud in her mouth. The sweet, dark liquid tasted like some kind of rare concoction, with a smooth delicacy whose fragrance delighted her senses.

"So this was the drink of Aztec kings," she said.

"It used to be," doña Ofelia said softly. "Now it is the drink of conquerers."

"Things we should put away," replied Serafina, placing the cup on the bench.

"Perhaps," the old lady said, taking a pouch of homegrown tobacco from under her blouse and slowly rolling the leaves into a dry corn leaf. When she had packed it tightly she held one end to the candle flame and lit the thick cigarette.

"Do you smoke?" she asked Serafina.

"Only during a ceremony."

"Ah, you're old-fashioned," doña Ofelia smiled. "Me, I have adopted the ways of the Españoles. When I was only a child, a raiding party of Apaches kidnapped me from my pueblo. Later they sold me as a slave. You know how it is, the Apaches come and steal the children of the Españoles, take their sheep and burn their fields. Then the Españoles attack them and take slaves. An eye for an eye, they say."

The old woman puffed on her cigarette and grew silent, perhaps thinking how different her life would be if she had grown up among her people.

"I was indentured to a family, and so I learned the ways of the Españoles. Then I came to work for the Governor. But there is another story. My first family used to say my father was Español. My mother from Picuris. When I was young I looked in the mirror and saw some features of the father I never knew. If that is true, how can I ask for my freedom from one or the other? I am both."

Serafina nodded. "Some of us have Spanish fathers."

"Ay. Too many Españoles came without wives. Nature is very strong. Throughout history, in all the corners of the earth, men have had their way with women. Conquerers impose themselves, children are born. Maybe nature is working something new in this land of our ancestors."

"But we must keep the ways of our ancestors," said Serafina.

"Yes. Our stories are as beautiful as the stories you tell the Governor. But those of us outside the circle are forgetting. We drink chocolate. We drink coffee. Foreign drinks. Who knows? In the future other people will come here and bring new drinks. I am an old woman. I love a cup of chocolate at night. Is that wrong?"

Serafina shook her head. It wasn't wrong for the old woman to enjoy this warm delicacy before sleep. But the more her people entered the world of the Españoles, the more of their customs they lost. Already they depended on sheep, cattle, pigs, iron pots, the fire of the forge where kitchen instruments were shaped. And the greatest desire of the men was to own and ride the horses of the Castillos.

Let us live like the Castillos, some said. Some became the genizaros, hispanicized Indians who gave up all of their native ways. They put the old ancestral spirits away and prayed to the Cristo on the cross. The saints became the new kachinas.

"No," Serafina whispered. "We will keep our ways."

"Ay, but I fear a blood bath coming," doña Ofelia replied. "Our men will rise up and cast the foreigners from our land. But what of me, and those like me? Do I go or stay? Maybe when there are enough of us mestizos we can lay equal claim to this earth, maybe then we do not have to choose."

"Only if we can meet each other as equals," Serafina said.

"Now I am a prisoner."

"You are a prisoner plotting freedom," doña Ofelia said. "With your stories," she added. "Do you realize the power you wield?"

"I made a wager with the Governor. If he likes my story he frees a prisoner. That is enough for me."

"You are a talented woman. The Governor listens to you."

"I do it for my people," Serafina replied.

"Your beauty attracts men. Young Gaspar has fallen in love with you."

Serafina blushed. She had never thought of herself as beautiful. For one woman to have more beauty than another was a foreign concept, an idea the Españoles thought meaningful. In her pueblo a woman was admired for the babies she could bring into the world, the bread she baked, the clay pots she molded, the firewood she gathered, her work in the corn fields, the gathering and putting aside of food for the winter. Ceremonies. Storytelling.

"I am a storyteller," she said. "I cannot help what he thinks of me."

Doña Ofelia looked at Serafina and nodded. Yes, the girl had a point. She did not know she was like a flower to a young man like Gaspar. Or the other young men of the villa who each morning came to watch the trials. In truth, they came to watch Serafina.

"Well, she said, you can confide in me. I will help."

She extinguished the stub of her cigarette, put the tobacco that was left back into her pouch, then rose slowly and picked up the quilted bedspread on Serafina's bed.

"I see you are working on the colcha."

"I thank you for lending me your sewing supplies and for the cloth you bring me."

The old woman held the colcha up to the light. There was no doubt; the girl was an expert seamstress. The stitches and pattern were unique. A golden sun rising.

"Working as hard as you do you will be done in a week," she said.

"I work all day, but I have no hurry," Serafina said.

Doña Ofelia put the colcha back on the bed and picked up the cup and candle.

"Good night, child. Sleep well."

"Thank you, señora. I truly appreciate your friendship."

The old woman left and Serafina blew out the candle. She covered herself with the thick buffalo robe and tried to sleep, but the soothing balm of night didn't come. Outside she heard Gaspar moving about, restless. He, too, could not sleep.

Was the Governor asleep? He said the stories reminded him of simpler childhood times. He seemed pleased with her, and she was beginning to trust him. He was a man of his word, like her father.

Serafina knew she had to concentrate on freeing the men and returning home. She thought of her parents. Her father was a strong-willed man and she his only daughter. She went everywhere with him, including the meetings where the elders discussed the harsh rule of the Castillos. This, she knew, was how she came to be named as one of the conspirators.

Her father had given her a silent signal as the soldiers led her away. Even now, she thought, he is camped in the hills above the villa, watching. He would fight before he let them send her to Zacatecas as a slave. Even now other men waited with him, and the only thing that kept them from attacking the villa was knowing the Governor was releasing the prisoners one at a time.

They must wonder if it meant a change in the heart of the Governor?

And her mother? Ah, she worried about her mother. Serafina knew she needed help at home. But her mother was also a strong woman who knew that the oppressive times they lived in called for many sacrifices.

Just then Serafina heard a coyote call. It was barely audible, but it was there, and then another. Her father and the men were somewhere in the hills. Their cries drove fear into those inhabitants who were not yet asleep.

Serafina pressed her ears against the wall. Yes, her father was calling from the hills. He was watching over her. She returned to her bed to sleep, a sleep full of dreams in which she mounted a horse and rode into the hills and freedom.

The Governor could not sleep either. He thought of the story of the Devil's godchild. The friars called the natives' dances the Devil's dances.

But the Governor didn't believe that. Serafina wasn't a creature of the Devil, but a creature of God. Her soul was pure, that was obvious. And yes, she had reason to resent the rule of the Governors.

In the morning when the prisoners were lined up he freed the prisoner as soon as Capitán Márquez finished his defense.

Again, a murmur surfaced in the crowd which had risen early to watch the proceedings. This was the fifth prisoner released; now the pattern was established.

The Governor paid no attention to the crowd. He went to the corrals, mounted his horse, and rode into the hills, returning worn and weary at sunset. He ate, tried to return to the don Quixote adventures he was reading, but he couldn't concentrate. Finally he rose, lit a candle and went to Serafina's room.

Hearing the knock she put aside the colcha, stood, and greeted him.

"How is the storyteller?" he asked, realizing he was glad to see her. When her hair fell around her shoulders she reminded him of his wife. How strange that a woman from Spain and a native should bear a resemblance to one another. Or was it only his imagination? Was it his desire for the children they never had that led him to see what was not there?

"Are you tired?" asked Serafina.

"Yes, it has been a hard day."

"You have many things on your mind. Decisions to make. You have to rest your body as well as your mind. Do the stories help?"

"Yes," he said, and smiled.

"Then sit and I'll tell you a story."

She took his hand and led him to the cot.

"Do you make the story fit the occasion?" he asked.

"Sometimes."

"Am I the character in the stories you tell?"

Serafina laughed, the first time she had felt enough at ease to laugh at the Governor. "You may be the actor in the story or not, as you wish."

"Perhaps that's the function of the cuentos, to allow us to see ourselves in the role of the actors. Like a play, or a mirror. But I talk too much. Begin and I will listen."

TWELVE

Marcos and María

here lived a widower in a faraway land who had two exceedingly beautiful and gifted children, Marcos and María.

It so happened these were very difficult times. There was a drought in the land, and invasions of locusts devoured what little vegetation the earth gave forth. Prophets roamed the land, predicting the end of time.

This man wanted to save his children, so he built a large underground room and filled it with provisions. There was enough food and water to last seven years. He kissed his children goodbye and buried them in the room.

At the end of seven years Marcos and María dug their way out of the subterranean room. Like Adam and Eve banished from the Garden, they found themselves alone in a desert.

The city they had known was gone. No trace of their father or neighbors remained. Only the blinding sun overhead warmed their bodies. They were innocents coming out into a brave new world.

—We must find a place for shelter, Marcos told María, and he led her to a mountain where they found a cave.

The two had spent so much time together that they promised never to leave each other. They would remain together forever, come what may.

The cave became their home, and they lived quite comfortably for many years. Marcos hunted rabbits and birds to sustain them. One particular day he climbed to the crest of the mountain and discovered a magnificent castle. He was about to venture in when he saw the giant who lived there. He crept away in fear and never climbed that path again.

A year later when Marcos was out hunting he found three cubs: a lion, a tiger, and a bear. He took them home and raised them, and when they were grown, they helped him hunt for food.

One day when Marcos was gone, the giant who lived on the mountain came down and found the cave. He looked inside and spied the lovely María. She was startled and asked him who he was.

—I am the ruler of the mountain, the giant replied. I live in a castle on the peak. I hold fiestas every night and invite my friends. We eat and dance all night.

María was intrigued. She remembered vaguely the fiestas her father had held when she was a child. Those were the fondest memories she had.

—What do you do here? asked the giant.

—I live with my brother. He hunts and I cook for him.

—A very boring life, said the giant. Come with me to my castle. I will marry you and provide you with all the pleasures of the world.

—I can't come with you, she replied. I promised my brother never to marry.

—So I will slay him, and you will be free of your promise. Ask your brother what path he will take tomorrow, and I will wait there to kill him.

María felt two emotions. One was the temptation of the pleasures the giant offered. He was a ruler who would care for her the rest of her life. She would sit like a queen by his side. The other emotion was fear. What would the giant do if she didn't do as he ordered?

—Very well, she finally said. I will do as you say.

The following day as Marcos was about to leave she asked which path he was taking. His animals had already warned him that she had told the giant what path he planned to take.

—Why do you ask me? You have never asked me before?

—I told the giant I will marry him, she replied.

—Ungrateful sister! roared Marcos. After all these years of taking care of you this is how you repay me! Very well, go with your giant. I am leaving, never to return.

He called to his animals and left.

The next day the giant arrived at the cave and asked María which way her brother had gone.

—I don't know, she replied. He was very angry and went away.

—No matter, said the giant. I'll find him.

He followed the trail until he spied Marcos. The giant attacked, but he was no match for the lion, the bear, and the tiger. They turned on the giant and killed him.

Sadly, Marcos looked back at the mountain that held the cave that had been his home. He loved his sister, but he knew he could never return. Their life would never be the same; she had betrayed him.

He traveled through many lands with his animals, until they came to the land of a great king. That morning as they walked down a canyon they found the king's daughter tied to a post.

—Why are you tied here, most beautiful lady? asked Marcos.

At first the princess was startled by the handsome man speaking to her, and equally afraid of the large tiger, bear, and lion that sniffed her shoes and the hem of her dress.

—There is a giant serpent that came to threaten my father's kingdom, she replied. It will destroy the kingdom and all its people unless my father offers me as hostage. Tonight the serpent will come for me.

—I will set you free, Marcos said.

—I warn you, the seven-headed serpent is enormous. It will kill you.

—I have very powerful friends, he said, pointing to his animals.

—If you free me, you will be my hero, said the princess.

Marcos turned to his animals.

—Go up into the canyon and wait for the serpent. You must kill it.

They went up the path and waited for the serpent. When the serpent arrived its loud cries echoed down the canyon, driving fear into all who heard it.

But the lion, the bear, and the tiger weren't afraid of the seven-headed serpent, whose mouths had razor-sharp teeth and long tongues that dripped with poison.

The bear, lion, and tiger attacked from all sides, clawing at the serpent's belly until they killed it. Then they returned to Marcos and told him the serpent was dead.

—You are free to return to your father, Marcos said to the lovely princess, but you must tell no one who freed you.

When the king's men found the princess they were overjoyed she was alive. They immediatedly took her to her father.

—Did the serpent come? he asked.

—It came, but a brave man killed it.

—Who?

—I do not know his name.

—I want to meet this brave man, and for saving your life I will give you to him as a wife.

It so happened that the next day a carbonero, a man who burns wood to make charcoal, found the dead serpent.

—They say the king will marry his daughter to the man who killed the serpent, he said to himself. I will claim her.

He cut the seven heads off the serpent and took them to the king.

—Ipa! he shouted. I am the man who killed the serpent!

—Then you shall marry my daughter, replied the king.

The princess grew sad. The carbonero had not saved her, and she did not want to marry him, but her father had made a promise that couldn't be broken. And she had promised the young man with the animals not to divulge his identity.

That day Marcos and his animals had found lodging with an old woman who lived on the outskirts of the village. She told Marcos a carbonero had killed the serpent and the king was marrying his daughter to the man. Lords and ladies and friends of the king would come from everywhere to attend the wedding.

—Would you like to eat the food of the fiesta? he asked her.

—Yes, but the poor are not invited.

Marcos turned to his tiger.

—Go to the dance and greet the princess. Don't return until she tells you to return. And don't bite anyone.

The tiger did as he was told. When he entered the dance hall everyone fled except the princess. Recognizing the tiger, she ran to him and stroked his head. Realizing he was hungry, she prepared a sack of the best meats and tied it to his neck. Then she told him to return to his master.

The tiger delivered the package and they all sat down to eat.

—Grandmother, would you like to sample some more of the wedding foods?

—Of course, my son. I am very hungry.

This time Marcos sent the lion with the same instructions he had given the tiger. As before, when the lion entered the dance hall everyone fled, including the carbonero.

The princess greeted the lion with great affection and sent him back with an even bigger package of food. Marcos, the old woman, and the animals ate every morsel.

—Grandmother? asked Marcos, are you still hungry?

—Oh yes, I could eat dessert.

Marcos sent the bear to the wedding feast, and the bear, who was a good dancer, even danced a waltz with the princess. He returned with an even larger package filled with cakes and sweets.

—Father, said the princess to the astonished king, have you seen the three animals that came to the fiesta?

—Yes, sputtered the king. But I don't know why they are so friendly to you.

—The man who is sending his animals to me is the one who saved me from the serpent, not the carbonero. Sending his animals to me means I can reveal him. The bear told me he stays in the hut of an old woman at the edge of the city.

—Go and bring this young man to me, the king told his guards. As for the carbonero, tie him to a wild horse and exile him from my kingdom.

The king's guards brought Marcos before the king.

—You saved my daughter and therefore she is yours to marry tomorrow.

—Will you have me? Marcos asked the princess.

—With all my heart, she replied.

The dancing continued all night and a happy Marcos and princess danced every dance together.

As it turned out, María was a serving maid working for the king. When she learned Marcos was to marry the princess she grew mad with jealousy. Hadn't Marcos long ago promised never to marry? The brother and sister had vowed to stay together.

And Marcos had killed the giant who had promised her many worldly pleasures. Why should he marry and enjoy life while she had no future?

She waited until he was alone in his room, knocked on his door, and entered. Marcos was overjoyed to see his sister. He invited her in, embracing and kissing her with love. He wanted to hear everything that had happened to her since he had left the cave.

After hours of listening to her story, he laid his head on her lap and fell asleep. Then María drew a large, magical pin she had hidden in her skirt and drove it into his skull. When she saw what she had done she was overcome with grief. She ran out of the castle, down to the river, crying out the name of her brother.

The next morning the king found Marcos dead, but he couldn't see the pin so he didn't know how the young man had died. When the princess heard the news she cried the entire day. Then she ordered a wake to be held so everyone would come and say goodbye to her savior, the man who was to be her husband.

In the stable the lion, bear, and tiger could be heard weeping for their master.

—It is time to take Marcos to church for his funeral, said the king. Release the animals so they can go up into the mountains. In a royal litter of gold we will carry Marcos to church.

When the animals were freed, instead of running for the mountains, they followed the funeral procession. When the princess sat with head bowed, the bear, lion, and tiger wept and licked Marcos's face, so great was their loss.

The bear held Marcos's head in his paws and stroked it. As he caressed his friend he discovered the head of the pin. He drew it out and Marcos opened his eyes.

—Thank you, kind friends, he said and rose from the gold litter. The animals cried with joy.

The princess ran to Marcos and embraced him.

The wedding was held and Marcos and the princess lived a long and happy life. Marcos took good care of the bear, lion, and tiger, his three magical friends.

María was never seen again, although often workers coming home late at night say they hear her weeping mournfully along the riverbank. Some say María is doing penance for betraying the love of her brother.

THIRTEEN

T he Governor sighed. "A tale of misguided love," he murmured, staring at the ceiling. "The cuentos of the people are exemplary. Sometimes even the most faithful lovers part. Something comes between them and not even love can withstand the feelings that erupt in the heart."

"If love is true, can it be destroyed by other emotions?" asked Serafina. She knew a little of the Castillos' concept of love, and the importance they attached to it intrigued her.

"I have read some of the writers of romances. Spain was full of writers who wrote of courtly love . . . that is, before Cervantes put a hole in their sails. Love is a theme in their poetry. Can it be true and strong and last forever? Ah, the romantic fabulists say yes. But in this case, the sister was tempted by the giant. The flesh is weak; she wanted the comfort, food, and fiestas the giant offered."

"What does the giant represent?" asked Serafina.

The Governor thought a moment. "Perhaps the Devil. He is powerful, and she is attracted to his power."

"But what if it's not the Devil?"

"Then it must be something in her own nature. She wants to be a queen. Seeking power is coupled with greed. I have seen those emotions affect both king and humble peasant. Those who came to the land of the Aztecs before us, the conqueror of Mexico himself, lusted for an empire. Once a man or a woman tastes power, he or she wants more and more."

"And you?" asked Serafina.

The Governor was, at first, startled by the question, but, yes, he thought, I have sought status.

"Yes. I confess I made my career a careful study. I came from a well-to-do family, received the best education in Spain, and returned to Mexico City with the new viceroy. I have courted favors, and returned favors, sought advancements—"

He paused. "I paid a price to become governor of New Mexico. My desire to be governor was so great I would have sacrificed anything. There were dozens of men in New Spain who wanted this post. Why not? Here one can create history. Be part of history. But every man must be part of his time, and exact from time his true destiny."

"Have you?" asked Serafna.

"I thought I had. Then things began to turn against me. My wife died, the drought came, the Apaches grew bolder in their raids—"

He stopped short.

"Why am I telling you this?"

"Perhaps there is no one else to trust."

"You are wise beyond your years, Serafina. Yes, whom can I trust? I have political enemies who say I am too much like Governor López. They make false reports to the Viceroy. Ah, why trouble you with my problems?"

He looked directly into her eyes, finding there the same soft gaze he remembered his wife's eyes held. An openness, a willingness to listen and understand.

"Perhaps you are right! I speak so openly because I feel I can trust you—"

Gathering courage he took the thought further. "I feel I can trust you like a daughter."

With that said he felt a relief, and her eyes told him she did not find the idea ridiculous.

"I would never reveal your feelings," she replied. "But a daughter I could never be. I must return to my family, my people."

"I understand," he said, standing and letting a soft sigh escape his lips. "But talking to you has been good for me. I confess that just days ago I wanted to leave this place. I looked forward to my term as governor ending so I could return to Mexico City. But now I am a changed man. I feel a new commitment. Something you have said, or something in the stories, tells me to stay and make this colony grow and thrive—"

He paused and looked at her. "But I impose too much. Forgive me."

No, she wanted to say, but checked herself. Their talks were not impositions at all, but something she had begun to cherish.

"It is late and I must excuse myself." He turned to go, pausing at the door. "Good night, Serafina."

"Good night, Your Excellency."

The door closed and Serafina returned to stitching her colcha. Moments later she heard someone talking to Gaspar, then a knock on the door.

"Enter," she said, and was surprised to see Capitán Márquez enter and close the door behind him.

"May I have a moment of your time?" the robust captain asked, standing at attention. Serafina noticed that his blonde beard and hair were slicked down with buffalo grease. The cotton shirt and trousers he wore were clean and pressed.

"How may I help you?" asked Serafina, standing.

"I am Capitán Antonio Márquez y Gómez," he replied, bowing slightly, awkwardly. "I have come to help you prepare your defense. If I may."

Serafina smiled. "I appreciate your offer, and what you have done for my countrymen, but do I need to plan a defense?"

"Yes, you do," he replied stepping forward. "You do not know the danger you're in. Granted, the Governor is your defender, I know that, but he is very distracted with the recent Apache raids. He's not aware of the new charges being planned against you."

"New charges? I don't understand."

"Ay, and a bundle of lies they are."

"Explain."

"Forgive me if I speak frankly, but I only have your best interest in mind. I want to help you."

"I thank you, but it is the Governor who must free the prisoners."

"Yes, and many of the people in the villa support the Governor's actions. The charges against the men are thin. It would be cruel punishment to send them as slaves to Zacatecas, to divorce them from their families forever. But with you it's different."

"How?"

"There is a small group of colonists who thoroughly hate the Governor. They feel that to keep the natives subdued they must be intimidated and punished harshly. These people say you have bewitched the Governor."

Serafina started to laugh, then looked closely at the captain's eyes. He was serious.

"They say I am a witch?"

"Yes."

"That's not true."

"That may be, but every whisper uttered in the villa is known. There is little to do in winter. People gossip, it gets exaggerated. Already a few men have gone to the prelate of the Holy Office of the Inquisition at Santo Domingo Pueblo. They will come to question you."

"But Fray Tomás has already questioned me. I prayed with him and he cleared me of any suspicion."

The captain stepped forward, and as he did the full beauty of Serafina was illuminated by the candle. He had two daughters her age, and when he had discussed Serafina's situation with them they had convinced their father that she was imprisoned falsely. It was they who pushed him to do something drastic. In short, he must help Serafina escape.

"The agent for the Inquisition will come to question others here in the villa, and there are some who hate the Governor enough to lie. Through their confessions the Inquisition will get to you. There is one man—" he paused momentarily. "One man who claims he followed the Governor when he rode into the hills. There, the man swears, the Governor took off his shirt and beat his back with thorny cactus. This is taken as a sign he is possessed."

Serafina turned away. She had noticed the Governor sat as if in great discomfort, but she had said nothing.

"It is common for penitents to perform such acts," Serafina finally said. "Some of the Catholics do this on Good Friday. What has the Governor's act of penance to do with me?"

"The Governor is not known for doing penance. So those who would destroy him say the strange behavior proves you have put a curse on him. That is why he is releasing the prisoners."

"What can I do about these false accusations?"

"Nothing. Fray Mateo, who is the agent of the Inquisition, will come to question you. He will call witnesses, and they will say the power you have over the Governor is demonic. There's only one solution."

"What?" she asked, holding her breath.

"You must escape."

"Escape?"

The word left her breathless. Of course this is what the pueblo children had been taught since childhood: when taken captive by the enemy, one plans to escape. Even now she knew that her father and friends were just outside the villa, keeping watch in the hills.

But the Governor was pardoning the men. The solution that had presented itself was far better than an attempt to escape which might jeopardize the lives of the other prisoners.

"But how? There is the guard—"

"Gaspar? He is with us. You see, I have two daughters. One of them will dress like you, and sit here in the evening. That will give us time to get to the horses."

"Us?"

"I will ride with you as far as Santa Clara. We know your people are waiting for you."

"But—"

"Please hear me out. I swear by the Bible and on my honor that I only wish you well. My family and I have discussed the escape. We only wish your freedom."

"But if you are found out you will be punished."

The captain nodded. "I am a poor captain in the service of His Most Royal Highness, the King of Spain. I have served well, I am honest. Yes, following the orders of my superiors I have led raids against your people. But my daughters, who have been present at the trials, have convinced me to take this step."

Serafina stood astonished. This was not a trap. The man was sincere. And he promised her freedom. What should she do?

"When would we go?"

"Tomorrow night. When we heard what they intend to do to you, we knew we had to act quickly."

"But they would send soldiers after us," she stammered. The idea of escape made her thoughts rush in many directions. Should she take the offer?

"No. I would be back here at the villa before morning. Believe me, it is better to die free than a prisoner of the Inquisition? You know what they can do."

Yes, she knew. Her family could be rounded up, sold as slaves. The pueblo itself would suffer as soldiers were ordered to destroy the kivas, the masks, all the holy objects of the elders. Would it not be better to flee?

"I cannot," she whispered.

"Why?"

"You have promised me deliverance. Anyone in my situation would gladly accept your offer. But I must stay until all the men are released and are safely back with their families."

The captain sighed. "You plead for their freedom, but who will plead for yours?"

"I must learn to defend myself," she answered.

The captain smiled. "Very well, if that's your decision. I will help if you allow me. I have little learning and less jurisprudence. But I will help."

"I thank you for the great risk you propose to take," Serafina said. "I thank you and your daughters."

"Ah, yes," the captain smiled. "As long as we have young people like them perhaps the future will be right. I wish you a good night."

"Good night, captain."

He bowed, turned, and left the room.

Serafina sat for a long time, thinking of the captain's offer. The freedom of the men meant more to her than her own. Finally, assured she had made the right choice, she snuffed out the candles, filling the room with the aroma of the burned wax, and slipped under the buffalo robe. In the dark winter night the coyotes called in the hills.

What a strange night, she thought. I have bewitched no one. Are the stories I tell bewitching? With this thought, she fell asleep.

In his room the Governor lay awake. He was beginning to see the thin line that separated the storyteller from the story. The stories Serafina told belonged to everyone, but whoever told the cuento could weave nuances into the plot. So at each telling something slightly new was woven into the story, and the audience responded as if the cuento was being told for the first time. The themes in the stories were like musical strings, and they played on the emotions of the listener.

But Serafina, ah, she belonged to no one. She belonged to her people because their welfare was her goal. Certainly she could never be the daughter he longed for. But having entertained the thought meant he had a certain kind of love toward her, a love expressing itself in the release of the prisoners.

We must love one another, he thought. That is the solution to our problems. Then he laughed. I, a man trained in war, thinking love will dissolve this animosity between us and the Pueblos? Yes, I can continue to show mercy toward the prisoners, but I must remain strong in my duty to protect the villa.

He awakened to a clear and warm morning, the kind of morning the Santa Feans called a blessing. The trial was perfunctory, the sixth prisoner quickly freed. The crowd gathered for the trial was smaller, as most people preferred to spend time gathering wood or hunting in the hills when the days were warm. The release of the prisoners had created a feeling of safety.

Children played in the plaza, women cooked meat, beans, and chile, and by noon the aroma of tortillas browning on comales filtered from the homes of the small villa of Santa Fé.

That evening the Governor knocked on Serafina's door in a very good mood. He had brought her a present.

"It is nothing," he said, "a brooch my wife wore. Please accept it as a token of friendship, a small reward for the stories you tell."

"Thank you, kind sir. In my culture we cannot refuse gifts, but I am not in a position to accept this one."

"I understand your situation, but this is the only way I have of thanking you."

Serafina looked into his eyes. He is sincere, she thought, and to refuse a gift, even from he who holds you prisoner, is contrary to our teaching. She took the brooch, a beautiful silver filigree with green stones that reflected the candle light.

"It is lovely," she said. "I thank you."

"Allow me," he said, taking the brooch and pinning it on her garment.

When he was finished he drew back. "It is the work of a famous silversmith from Toledo."

"In friendship," she whispered.

"Yes." He sat on the bench by the bed. "And tonight? What cuento have you to entertain me?"

"Whatever comes to mind," Serafina replied.

"You mean you don't plan or prepare the story ahead of time?"

"No. I tell whatever comes to mind."

"So there is no pattern to the storytelling . . ."

"Perhaps I relate what pleases me," she said, smiling. "A word, a stray thought, an emotion, or a sound awakens the story. The pattern is in the cuento itself, and in the listener."

"Ah." He smiled. "Very well, let's to the story."

Serafina sat on the cot and took up the colcha she was stitching. With work in hand and the candles glowing brightly, she began.

FOURTEEN

Two Compadres

Long ago there lived two compadres who were different in many ways. Vicente was an honest merchant who had acquired a small fortune. He thanked God for his good luck. His compadre Manuel was also a businessman, but envious of Vicente. Manuel thought Vicente had acquired his wealth with God's help.

Because there were thieves on the roads, they often traveled together for protection. One day they loaded their mules with goods and set out for Puerto de Luna. On the way they began to argue.

—Who profits more, asked Manuel, the man who rises early or the man whom God helps?

—The man whom God helps, replied Vicente.

—I don't trust in God, said Manuel. I have what I have because I work for it. Granted, you have more riches than I, but I still say I don't need God's help. Let's make a bet as to who is right, and the first three people we meet on the road will be our judges. If I win you must give me everything you own, and I will take out your eyes and leave you in the desert.

Vicente thought this was not a good bet to make, but he trusted in God. He would agree to the bet to teach his compadre a lesson, but he had no need for his compadre's goods. Certainly he would never think of blinding him.

The Devil who always traveled the road looking for an opportunity to grab a sinful soul overheard the bet. Here's my chance to take a man's soul, he thought. He quickly dressed as an honest man, mounted a horse, and rode toward the two compadres. They greeted him.

—Señor, said Manuel. My friend and I have a bet. Help us settle it. Who profits more in life, the man who gets up early to work or the man God helps?

The Devil could hardly bear to hear the name of God much less utter it.

—He who gets up early, he said and quickly rode away.

—I'm winning, said Manuel to Vicente.

Down the road the Devil appeared again dressed as a man carrying his goods on his back. The two compadres stopped him and explained the bet. Again the Devil said the man who gets up early profits.

—That's two votes for me, said Manuel.

Vicente was surprised. He knew the hard-working people of the region, and they all put their faith in God. Something was wrong.

Next the Devil appeared driving a fancy buggy. They asked him the same question and the Devil sputtered,

—Don't trust in God! Then he quickly rode away.

—I win, said Manuel. You must sign this paper giving me all your properties and fortune.

After Vicente signed the paper, Manuel came up behind him and put out his eyes.

Vicente cried in pain.

—Oh, cruel friend. I have given you everything I own. I didn't expect you would be so evil as to tear out my eyes.

—A bet's a bet, said Manuel. He took all of Vicente's mules and goods and hurried back to claim his properties, leaving his blind compadre alone.

Vicente suffered greatly. Even blinded as he was, he knew he had to find protection from the wild animals of the desert. Earlier he had spotted a tree along the road, and so as best he could he crawled round and round until he found the tree.

He climbed the tree and made ready to spend the night on the highest branches. Night fell and soon Vicente heard something approaching the tree.

It so happened this was a tree where three devils were accustomed to meeting. Beneath the tree they discussed the evil deeds they had done that day.

Trembling, Vicente overheard their conversation.

—How goes it? the first devil asked the other two.

—I'm doing very well, replied one. In the city down the road I have poisoned a young woman and she is slowly dying. She is the daughter of the king, and not even his best doctors can save her.

—How did you perform that good deed? asked one.

—I buried a horrible animal that looks like a toad seven feet under her bed. That animal is sucking her soul.

—Is there any way she can get well?

—Yes, if someone digs out the animal and kills it. Then she will instantly have her health again. But what about you? What are you up to?

—I have a kingdom in my claws, said the second devil. I have dried up all their rivers and springs. They have no water to drink and are dying of thirst.

—How did you put that curse on the land? And can it be taken away?

—Up the river from the city there's a gigantic white boulder on the hill. I have locked up the waters in the boulder. If someone could break open the boulder, then the waters would flow again.

—And you? they asked the third devil.

—Oh, I had a good day. I served three times as a judge.

—How did you do that?

The devil explained the two compadres' bet and how he had served as judge. When he finished his story one of the devils praised his deception.

—You win as deceiver of the day, one said.

—I appreciate the honor. But let me tell you more. The poor man doesn't know that at the foot of this tree there's a magic spring. He has only to wash his eyes with the water and his sight will be restored. But no telling where he is by now.

The devils finished their conversation and left. When he was sure he was alone, Vicente climbed down from the tree and crawled around searching for the spring. When he found it, he bathed his eyes and instantly his sight was restored.

—Thanks be to God, who reveals the devils' work, he said.

The next day he set out for the city where the king's daughter lay ill. At the edge of the city he found a kind old woman who gave him food and a room in which to sleep.

When he was rested he sent the old woman with a message to the king.

—Tell the king I can cure his daughter.

The old woman went running to the king and told him a man lived in her home who claimed he could cure the princess.

—Bring him to me, said the king. If he cures my daughter I will give him half of my kingdom.

The old woman returned to Vicente. He went immediately to the king.

—Are you the man who can cure my daughter? asked the king.

—Yes.

—Make her well and I will give you half of all I own. Tell me what medicines you use?

—I don't use medicine, replied Vicente. I only need four strong young men with picks and shovels.

The king ordered four men to go with Vicente to the princess's room. She lay in a coma, near death. Vicente ordered the bed moved and had the men break the floor and dig. They earth was as hard as rock, but Vicente urged them to keep digging.

When they were seven feet down they encountered the ugly animal that had been sucking the princess's soul. The evil thing hissed and jumped at Vicente, but he killed it with his shovel. Then he took it outside and burned it.

When this was done the princess opened her eyes and spoke. The king and queen were overcome with joy. Within hours the princess was walking and talking, completely cured.

The king offered Vicente half of his kingdom, but Vicente said that that must wait. He was going to the next kingdom to help the people dying of thirst. Before he left he asked that the king take care of the old woman who had fed him.

When he arrived at the drought-stricken city, he found lodging for the night at the hut of an old crone. She told him about the terrible conditions.

—All our animals have died. The people travel three days to bring water in barrels. The king has sent his troops to dig for water in the mountains, but they find nothing.

—What would the king give to someone who can make the rivers flow? asked Vicente.

—Oh, he would make that person a rich man.

—Very well, go tell the king I can release the waters of the rivers.

Early next morning the old woman did as she was told.

—Bring him to me, said the king. My people cannot last without water one more day.

So Vicente appeared before the king.

—Are you the man who claims he can make the rivers run again?

—Yes, your majesty, I am.

—If you can do that you can have whatever you desire in my kingdom. You will have all the money you ask for.

—Agreed, said Vicente. You can help me by providing me with twelve young men with steel picks and hoes.

The king ordered everything loaded on horse-drawn carts, and Vicente and the men started up the mountain. When they found the huge white boulder Vicente ordered the men to break it apart.

The work was difficult and long, but finally they split the boulder and the waters of the river gushed out.

When they returned to the city the king and musicians greeted Vicente. There was great rejoicing.

—Stay with us and marry my daughter, said the very grateful king.

—I have a family to return to, replied Vicente. You can pay me what you wish.

The following day the king had two mules loaded with gold and Vicente returned to the city where he had cured the princess. This king was equally generous. He had three mules loaded with sacks of gold and he sent soldiers to accompany Vicente home.

When Vicente returned to his city, he learned from his wife that Manuel had taken all his possessions and thrown her out in the street.

Quickly the news spread throughout the city that Vicente had returned. Friends came to see him and rejoice that he was alive.

Vicente bought a lot of land with farms and cattle, and he paid with gold.

Manuel learned that his compadre had returned, and that he was very rich. He couldn't believe it, so he went to see him.

—Compadre, he said, are you the same one I blinded and left in the desert?

—Yes, replied Vicente. You have treated me very cruelly. But thanks to God I survived and prospered.

—But how did you come into this great wealth? asked the envious and greedy Manuel.

—I found a tree nearby and climbed it. That night thieves came and hid the gold they had stolen at the foot of the tree. When they left I climbed down and took as much gold as I wanted. Anyone can climb that tree and then take the gold.

—Take me to that place, begged Manuel.

—I cannot. Go by yourself, I will not go with you. Besides, you have to be blind, as I was, to find the tree.

—Then I beg you to take me there and blind me.

—That would be criminal, said Vicente. I cannot do what you did to me.

But Manuel's greed was overwhelming.

—I will sign a paper returning all of your property, he insisted. And hold you blameless. But you must blind me. You are my compadre and you must do as I say.

Vicente relented. He took Manuel to the desert and put out his eyes. Then he returned home, leaving Manuel to crawl in search of the tree. When he found it he was overjoyed. He climbed it and sat on a high branch to wait for the thieves.

When he heard someone nearing the tree he was sure he was going to be a man far richer then Vicente. He didn't know it was the three devils who had come to their reunion under the tree.

The devils began to talk about their day's adventures and Manuel listened intently.

—I did very well today, said the first devil. I have two kingdoms at each other's throats. Soon they will destroy each other.

—I also did very well, said the second devil. I sent a giant serpent to destroy a city. There is nothing the king can do. Soon the city will fall into my hands.

The third devil heard something move in the branches and looked up.

—Well, he said. I think I've done better than both of you. Look what I've found!

He reached up, grabbed Manuel, and in a flash they took him with them to a hot and dismal place.

he Governor smiled when Serafina had finished the story. Except for the discomfort of his back, he had relaxed as she told the story.

So, he thought, the bad compadre was gobbled up by the Devil. His greed earned him an eternity in hell.

Compadres were like brothers, they were supposed to take care of each other. His own compadre, don Roberto, had remained in Mexico City, turning down the offer to start a new life in la Nueva México.

As he thought of his compadre and his comfortable home in the capital of New Spain, the Governor sighed. Perhaps Roberto had been the wiser. The capital was now a civilized city. Music, art, and dance were flowing in from Spain. Representatives from the European capitals came to do business. A whole new way of life was flourishing in land Hernán Cortés had conquered, a new façade lay over the civilization and arts of the Aztecs.

Here, there was little by way of culture—a few books, the cuentos, and the church services to lift the spirits. Once a year on January 25 the villa celebrated the feast day of St. Paul, the patron saint, then the soldiers and citizens reenacted the old drama *Los Moros y los Cristianos*. Dressed in their breastplates and helmets and brandishing swords made from fine Toledo steel, the soldiers on prancing horses presented a wonderful spectacle.

The natives came from the pueblos to watch. Clearly they saw in the vanquishing of the Moors by the Christian knights the same power His Majesty's rule held over the Pueblos. The play was drama and entertainment, but it also presented a message. The Moors had been defeated in Spain in 1492, the Pueblos had given in to coexistence in 1598 when Oñate colonized their lands.

But the Pueblos still kept their ways; they continued to hold their Kachina dances. The prior Governor López had told the ecclesiastical authorities the natives were allowed to hold the Kachina dances. This infuriated the Franciscan friars, and gave the Pueblos a breath of freedom. Fray Alonso Posada, then newly assigned prelate and agent of the Inquisition, opposed Governor López and sought to stop the Kachina dances. López laughed in his face, and the dances continued.

Posada filed charges against López, who was tried by the Tribunal of the Holy Office of the Inquisition in Mexico City and found innocent. The friars of New Mexico had failed to show the dances were idolatrous or demonic. The governor who succeeded López, Peñalosa, was also attacked by Posada, setting the stage for a continuing conflict between church and civil authorities over who held jurisdiction over the natives of New Mexico.

The Governor wondered whether it would not have been wiser to allow the natives to continue with their ceremonies. He glanced at Serafina. When she finished her story her custom was to remain silent, stitching the pieces of cloth that were becoming a rich-textured colcha. Was there a pattern in the blanket? He peered intently. Yes, probably the same symbols they used on their clay pots and ceremonial kivas.

He had been in a kiva once. According to the natives the kiva was the pueblo's church. Descending by way of a ladder, he had found it brilliantly decorated with fine, colorful murals. By the light of the fire in the middle of the kiva he could see these people were gifted artists. But he couldn't understand the meaning of the murals. He was told the paintings honored the ancestors, transcendent beings, rain people, corn maidens, and the mother earth they so adored.

They come to pray at our church, thought the Governor. Why can't I go and pray at theirs? Some of our people attend the Kachina dances. We all adore God in different ways. Why can't we respect the Pueblo way?

He looked at Serafina. How comfortable he felt with her tonight! He admired her talents as a storyteller and weaver. She could pray at church and in her pueblo way. She had learned to incorporate the two.

Maybe the friars are making a mistake in not allowing the native ceremonies to continue, he thought.

But in his heart he felt there was only one faith, one right religion, and the Christian duty was to baptize all heathens into the church.

Would Serafina give up her religion? No, that was part of her. Would she give up protesting the Governor's rule? That was the unanswered question.

One day she would make a man a good wife. She was strong, intelligent, surely good at all housekeeping chores. What man wouldn't feel honored to sit at home on winter evenings and listen to her cuentos? What father wouldn't adore the beauty of his daughter and her gifts?

"You are quiet tonight," said Serafina, putting the colcha aside.

"Your stories make me think," he replied.

"What is in your mind?"

"I was thinking of my compadre don Roberto. A fine and honest man. He lives in Mexico City, the capital of Nueva España. I miss his companionship. Here I have no compadre, no one with whom to share my thoughts. Once I could talk to my wife . . ."

"How did she die?"

"Last winter. Many died from the terrible cold that afflicted us. She had a gentle nature. She took sick and within a week she was gone."

"Do you miss her?"

"Oh, very much. At first I was lonely. But I had my work to do, keeping the colony together. So much to do in relation to your people—"

"A great responsibility."

"Yes. But I feel up to the task. I am Vicente of tonight's story. A good compadre." He smiled and looked into Serafina's bright, dark eyes.

"But even Vicente lies," she reminded him. "He tells Manuel that it is a thieves' fortune that is hidden under the tree."

"Ay, there's the rub. Human nature gets in the way, always confounding us."

"Would you blind your compadre?"

"No, never."

"Would you blind anyone?"

"No, it's inhuman."

"Would you whip or hang a man?"

Ah, thought the Governor, she's referring to Governor Treviño who, not long ago, hanged three Tewa Indians accused of witchcraft. A fourth man had hung himself, and forty-three others were either beaten or imprisoned. The event had almost precipitated a rebellion, and the memory of the incident was inciting much of the current unrest.

"Treason has to be punished. It is a crime against society. If left unpunished, the social fabric breaks down, the rule of law collapses."

"Is it treason to hold our own beliefs, to want to throw off the yoke of slavery?"

"You are not slaves. You have your pueblo, your lands to farm."

"But we must pay tribute, and answer to the friars."

"Those things are necessary for our survival," replied the Governor.

With this said both fell into silence. Each knew the arguments, and each came from such a different point of view, a different world. What could heal the wounds? Respect for each other's views, kindness, a forgiveness for past atrocities committed?

"You're not comfortable," she said, noticing again the way he kept his back away from the chair.

"It's nothing. A sore back. I took a fall from my horse."

"Take off your shirt and let me see."

"No. I insist, it's nothing. Don't trouble yourself."

"But I want to help you." She went to the pantry and brought out a small clay bowl. "I have an ointment I made for my hands. Dry mint leaves, ground osha boiled with the sap of the piñon tree."

Reluctantly he removed his shirt, exposing bruises along his back.

"It's nothing, a few scratches," he explained.

"This will help," she said as she rubbed the balm into the welts.

The ointment relieved the pain. Her fingers gently and deftly spread the soothing cream along his back.

"There," she said and handed him his shirt.

"I am grateful. Thank you. The irritation is gone. You have some knowledge of healing balms and herbs."

"My mother is a healer," Serafina replied. "As are many of the women of my pueblo. I learned from her."

"I know I will sleep well. And I have you to thank."

He wanted to go on talking to her, enjoying her company, perhaps learn more about her life in the pueblo.

"I'm afraid I've overstayed my visit. I must say good night."

"Good night, Your Excellency."

"Thank you again for the unguente. I hope it hasn't been too much trouble."

"Not at all."

"I feel," he began, "I can't tell you how I feel. Grateful. There are so many things to talk about—Come early tomorrow night. We can have dinner together."

"Thank you, Your Excellency, but I can eat only what the other prisoners eat."

"Then I will have doña Ofelia feed your kinsmen what we eat. Fresh venison, eggs and chile. We have turkeys she can broil. And those wonderful wheat tortillas she is so famous for. And apple pies for dessert. She has an excellent store of dried apple slices. I will have the same meal sent to the other prisoners. So you cannot refuse."

"As you wish, Your Excellency."

"Very well, until tomorrow." He took her hand. "Good night."

"Good night, Your Excellency."

He bowed and left, Serafina returned to her work, but she had barely picked up the colcha when doña Ofelia knocked and entered.

"Is the Governor gone?" she asked.

"Yes," replied Serafina.

"Ah, you look beautiful tonight, hija," said the old woman, placing her candle and the cup of chocolate on the table.

"I do not think myself beautiful," Serafina replied.

"Still, the fair-skinned Españoles like your long, black hair, those eyes like dark night that reflect stars, your skin bronzed by the sun. Yes, the Castillos like our women. So many of the soldiers, like the young Gaspar, have married our women."

Serafina looked at doña Ofelia. What was she getting at?

"Drink your chocolate, child," she said, then mumbling to herself she turned and went out, shutting the door behind her.

The next morning a strange rumbling filled the skies over the Villa de la Santa Fé. Clouds swept down from the north, covering the mountain peaks with a swirling mantle of snow. In the lower elevations a fine drizzle fell.

In spite of the rain many of the citizens lined the plaza for the day's trial. The land had been suffering a long drought, and many thought this January rain presaged a good spring. Perhaps the drought was breaking. There was nothing better for the corn, wheat, chile, and other vegetables that were grown along the Río Grande valley than rain from the heavens.

The old men who kept the caniculas, the forecasting of the year's weather by studying the weather of the first twelve days of January, nodded with satisfaction. They had noted the weather of the first twelve days; the weather of each day corresponded to the weather of the twelve months. It was a system used for predicting weather by the farmers.

The Governor seemed in especially high spirits. He looked at Serafina and smiled, then he greeted those waiting under the portal. Seeing the prisoners standing in the rain without adequate wraps he ordered his maese de campo to provide them with buffalo robes.

He turned and greeted those assembled to watch the proceedings. "A fine day," he said, "with just the rain we need for spring. Let us pray for a bountiful summer."

He nodded at Fray Tomás who stepped forward and said a prayer of thanksgiving. Then the Governor motioned for the trial of the seventh prisoner to begin, and as was predicted, the prisoner was freed. For the first time a few in the crowd applauded. Perhaps, the citizens of the villa thought, the Governor is doing the right thing, and a new era of peace will reign.

That evening the Governor's room was as brightly lit as it had been for Christmas. A crackling fire warmed the room. Candles blazed on hearth and table, lending the room a festive feeling.

The Governor, his hair and beard neatly trimmed, nearly drove doña Ofelia crazy with his orders that every detail be just right. Dressed in his best cotton pantaloons, a silk shirt and wool vest, he reveled in the new-found joy he took in hosting the meal.

"Doña Ofelia," he confided, "is it possible that a single man could adopt a daughter?"

Doña Ofelia understood his meaning but said nothing. She shook her head and went on about her business.

The Governor shrugged and opened a bottle of wine. A case, a special gift from don Roberto, sent up the Camino Reál from Mexico City. A stout red. Yes, México was beginning to produce good wine. As was the colony, for already in Santo Domingo and further south in the hacienda of don Bernal, the friars cultivated their vineyards and pressed some excellent wines.

A knock at the door startled the Governor. Gaspar opened the door and in stepped Serafina. She looked like a princess in the white lace gown. Her long black hair glistened as it cascaded over her shoulders.

"Come," said the Governor, extending his arm to lead Serafina to the table, not noticing Gaspar's drawn face. The young soldier closed the door with a sigh.

They ate in silence, a silence broken only by doña Ofelia as she served pea soup, goat cheese, then slices of fresh venison covered with a red chile sauce, and the warm tortillas which lent an aroma to the meal.

After the meal they sat by the fireplace, the Governor sipping coffee while he listened to Serafina's story.

SIXTEEN

The Tree That Sings

One afternoon, as the king took his walk, he heard laughter coming from an open window. He paused to look inside. He saw three sisters laughing and talking.

—I would like to marry the king's keeper of wines so I could drink all the fine wines, the eldest said.

—I would like to marry the king's baker, said the middle sister, so I could eat all the good bread.

—I would like to marry the king, said the youngest, whose name was Estella. Then I would have everything I need.

The king fell in love with the youngest sister, and when he returned to his palace he sent his servants for the sisters. When they stood before him he granted their wishes.

—You wanted to marry my wine steward, he said to the eldest. It shall be granted.

—No, no, the sister protested, I was just joking.

—Your wish will come true, the king insisted. And you wanted to marry my baker, he said to the middle sister.

—No, no, we were just playing, she protested.

—Nevertheless, you will marry the baker, said the king. And you shall marry me, he said to Estella.

And so all three were married, as the king decreed.

The two sisters were furious that they had to work all day with their husbands and never got to taste the bread or the wine. On the other hand, Estella and the king were very happy.

Months later the king had to go very far away to fight a war. Shortly after he was gone Estella had a baby. The two jealous sisters came to tend Estella. The took the baby boy and threw him into the pig pen, and they put a puppy in the crib.

The gardener was passing by the pig pen and heard the baby crying. He took it home where he and his wife took care of the baby, whom they baptized Juan.

Estella was shocked to find the puppy in the crib, but she accepted her fate as God's will. When the king returned he too was surprised.

—If it it God's will we have a dog, then let it be so, he said. He loved his wife as much as ever, something the two jealous sisters couldn't understand.

A year later Estella was pregnant again. At this same time, the king had to go fight another war. Estella delivered a baby boy, and before she could hold it the two sisters took it away and put a kitten in its place.

They threw the baby into the pig pen. The gardener happened by before the pigs could harm the baby, and he took it home and baptized it Pedro.

The two sisters wrote the king to hurry home, writing that Estella had delivered a kitten.

When the king returned home he laughed joyfully. He and Estella didn't understand what was happening, but they gave thanks anyway.

The two envious sisters pulled their hair and plotted to destroy the love between Estella and the king.

They waited until the king went away again. When Estella delivered her third child the two sisters took the baby girl away and threw her in the pig pen. They put a piece of rotten meat in the crib.

The gardener found the baby girl and took her home. He and his wife baptized her Pervís.

When Estella found the piece of meat in the crib she was horrified. So was the king when he returned.

—You have deceived me three times, said the king to Estella. But this time you have gone too far!

He ordered a glass house be built and he banished his wife to live there. Then he ordered all the people to pass by the glass house and insult Estella.

Many years later the gardener and his wife died. Juan, Pedro and Pervís continued to live in the house. They had learned gardening from their father, so they kept the most beautiful garden in the city.

One day an old woman stopped to admire the garden.

—How are you, granddaughter? she greeted Pervís. What a beautiful house you have! And what a lovely garden. It only lacks three things to be more beautiful than the king's gardens.

Pervís grew curious.

—What are those things? she asked.

—Haven't you heard the story of the bird that can speak, the tree that sings, and the water of gold?

—I have, replied Pervís, but it is a fantasy.

—No, they exist in a dangerous place on top of the Mountain of the East.

With that the old woman grinned and hobbled away.

When Pervís's brothers returned from work she told them what the old woman had said.

—With those things we would be richer than the king, said Juan. I am the oldest, so I will go in search of them.

The following morning he packed provisions and saddled his horse. He gave his sword to Pervís.

—If I have bad luck and do not return you will know because my sword will bleed.

Juan traveled to the Mountain of the East and there met a hermit. He asked the hermit for directions, but the old man had such a long, thick beard Juan couldn't understand what he said. He took a pair of scissors and cut off the hermit's beard.

—I am looking for the bird that speaks, the tree that sings, and the water of gold.

—It is a very dangerous place, replied the angry hermit. Many kings and princes have gone up the mountain in search of those things, and none have returned.

—I will succeed, Juan insisted. You must help me.

—Take this magic ball and roll it. Follow it until it stops. There you will find what you seek.

Juan rolled the ball and followed it until it stopped in front of an ominous field of boulders. Juan shivered. All around him strange figures of man-sized rocks rose from the earth.

Suddenly a dreadful voice called out.

—There he is! Grab him and kill him!

Before Juan could run away the evil spirit turned him into a rock.

Back home the sword he had given Pervís began to bleed, and she and Pedro knew their brother was dead.

—I must go at once, said the grief-stricken Pedro. Take my knife, he told Pervís. If spots of blood appear on it you will know I am dead.

He rode full speed toward the Mountains of the East. When he arrived he met the hermit.

—I am looking for my brother who came in search of the bird that speaks, the tree that sings, and the water of gold.

—Oh, the one who cut my beard. I wouldn't search for him if I were you.

—I will go and you must help me, insisted Pedro.

—Very well. Take this magic ball and follow it until it stops. There you will find your brother.

Pedro rolled the ball along the path until it stopped at the foot of a mountain. He got down from his horse and began to climb.

—There he is! the voice shouted. Grab him and kill him!

Pedro turned to flee and as he did so he became a rock.

At home Pervís saw drops of blood appear on the knife.

—Now both my dear brothers are missing, she cried. I must find them.

She mounted her horse and rode toward the Mountain of the East in search of her brothers. On the road she met the hermit and inquired if he had seen two young men in search of the bird that speaks, the tree that sings, and the water of gold.

—Yes, I saw the two. They went up the mountain but did not return.

—I will look for them, said Pervís.

—It is a dangerous place, the old man warned her. There are evil voices that create an enchantment. No one returns from their spell.

—Voices? said Pervís. It must be the bird that speaks that lays the spell. That is the secret. I will cover my ears with wool.

—You are truly wise, said the hermit. Take this magic ball and roll it along the path. Where it stops you will find what you seek.

Pervís filled her ears with wool then followed the ball up the path. Where it stopped she saw the strange rocks that looked like humans, and near the rocks was perched the bird that speaks.

—Grab her and put a spell on her, said the bird, but Pervís could not hear the incantation.

Instead she grabbed the bird and held it tight. She took the wool out of her ears and spoke to the bird.

—Magical bird, now you are my prisoner and must do as I command. Where is the tree that sings and the water that is gold?

—There! cried the frightened bird.

Pervís looked and saw the water that ran like gold. She heard the sweet melody of the tree.

—How can I take them with me?

—Take a branch from the tree and plant it at home. It will grow. Take water in a bottle. When you come to the rocks that look like humans, sprinkle them with this magical water.

Pervís did as she was told. She sprinkled a drop of water on each rock and as she did her brothers emerged from the rocks, as did other men once held prisoners. They greeted each other with joy and tears.

The three went home and Pervís planted the branch, which grew into a lovely singing tree. Its melodies wafted out like rainbows across the valley. The water in the bottle became a spring gushing gold.

A few days later, while Juan and Pedro were hunting in the mountain, they met the king. The king was impressed by the brothers' hunting skills, and he invited them to visit him at his palace.

Juan and Pedro visited the king, who was extremely pleased with their company. They in turn invited the king to visit their home, which he promised to do.

When the brothers told Pervís the king was coming to dinner she didn't know what to serve. She asked the bird what she should feed the king.

—Bake him a pie of pearls, replied the bird.

Pervís did as she was told. When the king arrived he was astounded at the beauty of the gardens, the singing tree, and the water of gold. He did not see the bird which hid itself behind some leaves.

Pervís served the pie and when the king bit into it he discovered the pearls.

—Is it possible that a king should eat pearls? he asked.

From his hiding place the bird replied.

—Is it possible that a woman should give birth to a dog and a cat?

—Who said that? cried the startled king. He was even more astounded when he turned and saw the bird which spoke to him.

—Your wife's envious sisters are the ones who replaced your children with a dog, a cat, and rotten meat. These three are your real children.

The king was overjoyed with the revelation. He took Juan, Pedro and Pervís to his palace, and he sent for his wife and asked her pardon.

The family was reunited, except for the evil sisters who had tricked the king. He ordered that they be dragged by horses into the desert.

n evening could not be more perfect, thought the Governor as Serafina finished her story. Contentment filled his heart.

"I remember that story from my childhood," he murmured. "The sisters are envious of Estella. Envy is a monster in the heart."

"My mother taught me many stories," replied Serafina. "Now the stories mean freedom to my countrymen."

"And if you did not have the motive of their freedom, would your stories be as enchanting?"

"I would hope so. The story is sacred in my culture. Winter is the time for telling stories."

"But these are Spanish cuentos, tales I heard as a child. Do you ever tell the stories of your people?"

"It is not permitted," replied Serafina. "We can tell hunting and farming tales, those that describe everyday experiences. But we cannot tell stories about our tradition."

"Why?"

"The friars say our stories are pagan."

"Yes, and so are the Greek myths we tell our children to this day," said the Governor. "Perhaps we judge your people too harshly."

"Some even call our stories works of the Devil. They force us not to repeat them. Don't they know we would lose the culture of our ancestors if we didn't tell their stories?"

"Lose your culture," the Governor repeated thoughtfully. "Yes, you're right. If a culture forgets the stories of its ancestors then it dies. The Greeks are remembered because they passed their myths on to the Romans, and they passed them on to us. Those myths inspire our art and music, and the new stories that spring from ancient legends."

He paused, then added, "Why can't we allow your stories to exist?"

"As you know, the friars are opposed to our Kachina dances," Serafina answered. "When your people first came to our land we told the stories of our creation, the coming forth from the sipapu. But they told us we must not believe such stories. So now we keep our religion to ourselves."

"Someday perhaps you can tell me the stories of your people. These winter nights are so long. The rain has changed to snow."

Serafina rose. "I am tired. I thank you for the dinner, but it is time for me to rest."

"I understand," said the Governor, rising.

He knew that it wasn't right for him to keep her beyond the dinner hour. He had gotten to know her well these past eight nights, and he respected their agreement.

Here was no ordinary young woman. She was gifted. Dressed as she was tonight her beauty could vie with the ladies in any court in Europe. In the capital of New Spain she would be called an Aztec princess.

"Our agreement is for you to tell one story," he said with some sadness.

"Yes," she replied.

"I can't help thinking that perhaps one day this land will be like the garden in your story. The tree will sing with many voices, the birds will speak the truth, and the river of gold will nourish our fields."

"We will pray for that," Serafina said,

He went to the door and called doña Ofelia, who instantly appeared, holding a lighted candle.

"Please escort Serafina to her room," he said.

Doña Ofelia nodded. "Yes, Your Excellency."

"Good night, Serafina."

"Good night, Your Excellency," she replied and went out.

The minute the door closed behind them doña Ofelia held the candle close to Serafina and whispered.

"You have a vistor."

"Who?"

"Fray Tomás. And he is in a nervous state. Come."

She led Serafina through the dark, low-ceilinged rooms of the residence, muttering as she went. "You have stirred up a hornet's nest. Some of the people like what the Governor is doing, others don't. The enemies say the Governor is enchanted by you."

Serafina frowned. "The witchcraft accusations are silly."

"Yes, but they have spies everywhere. You must be careful. Every step is fraught with danger. Listen to the friar, he is a holy man."

She paused only when they arrived at Serafina's door. "I sent Gaspar to the kitchen to eat his supper. I will remain outside your door, to give warning if anyone comes. Oh, what a terrible world we live in. There is a storm coming."

Serafina knew the storm doña Ofelia alluded to was not the snow that had arrived. Something ominous was in the air, and the old woman was worried. Else why would she stand guard?

"Thank you, doña Ofelia," Serafina whispered, then opened the door and went in. Fray Tomás, who had obviously been pacing, turned to greet her.

"Serafina. Buenas noches."

"Buenas noches, Fray Tomás. Please sit. Tell me, to what do I owe this visit?"

She felt the anxiety of the friar. His hair was unkempt; he had come in a hurry. On the cot lay a small bundle. What? Serafina wondered.

"Haven't you heard?"

"Heard what?"

He paused and looked closely at her. "Your dress," he stuttered. "You look lovely."

"Thank you, Fray Tómas."

Realizing what he had said the friar blushed. "Forgive me. The intent of my words is to convey the beauty of your soul, your inner light."

"I understand," replied Serafina. "But please sit down and tell me what brings you out in this snowstorm."

"I can't sit. I'm too agitated. It's obvious you haven't heard. But surely the Governor must be aware—"

"Aware of what?"

"An indio, one of your people, rode in from Santo Domingo just moments ago."

"Who?"

"He didn't give his name. Only that he was a friend. Then he disappeared back into the storm. The poor man was nearly frozen. The snowstorm caught him at La Bajada. He came directly to me, hoping I could help. The Inquisition has decided to question you."

"I don't understand," Serafina said.

"The messenger said the prelate and agent for the Inquisition has chosen Fray Mateo and two others to come and question you. If the snow hadn't fallen they would be here now. But tomorrow, or the day after, as soon as the storm clears, they will come."

Serafina shrugged and let out a deep sigh. "They have no jurisdiction over me," she said.

"True, the Inquisition has no charge over the natives, but they see you as a threat. They can get others to testify."

"You mean to raise lies against me."

"Yes. Anything to prove you practice witchcraft. They can send you to Mexico City to the tribunal. You see, if they can get rid of you they can topple the Governor."

"But I'm not a witch. You said so yourself. You questioned me."

"I know you're not a witch, but I'm not a member of the committee. I now know the names of the three friars chosen to interrogate you. Fray Mateo has been the most agressive in stamping out your kachina dances and all forms of your religion. In front of him you will be like a lamb led to slaughter."

"The Governor will protect me," Serafina blurted out.

"Yes, he will protect you," agreed the friar. "But there will be a protracted battle. The church wants the right to tell the civil authorities that it alone is in charge of your people. This battle between the church and secular authorities has been intense since Governor López was charged by the Fray Posada. There is no love lost on either side. If this committee can prove the Governor has consorted with a witch, they will have won the battle."

"I have not consorted with the Governor!" Serafina snapped back.

"I meant no disrespect. But the people know it is because of you the prisoners are freed. Perhaps he means well, but he doesn't realize that by his actions he compromises you. And himself. His enemies will use his relationship with you against him. Against you."

"How?"

"They will produce witnesses, those closest to you."

"Who?"

The friar went to the door and listened. Then he turned to Serafina and whispered. "The old woman."

"Doña Ofelia? No."

"You trust her, I know. But a committee of the Inquisition can frighten the hardiest soul into confessions. You don't understand the political ramifications. Your people are ready for a revolution. Everybody knows that. That's why you were taken prisoner. The civil authorities and the church are locked in battle to win control of the Pueblos, and you have become the pawn."

"A pawn in the struggle between your civil authorities and the Franciscans! Don't you know the only thing my people want is to be left in peace? To continue our way as we have since we first came to this earth?"

"I know, my child, but you have no power. The Governor might protect you, to a point, but he also has to protect his position. What if he decides to desert you?"

Serafina gasped. The Governor had become like a second father to her, a man she could trust. She had never thought he would desert her.

"Every Governor remembers the first governor of la Nueva Mexico, don Juan de Oñate," continued Fray Tomás. "What he did resulted in his leaving office in disgrace. He spent years and a fortune clearing his name. Those who have served since then remember history."

Serafina nodded.

"Do you understand?" the friar asked.

"Yes."

"Then there is only one solution. You must flee."

"Run away? When?"

"Tonight." He reached for the bundle on the cot. "I brought one of my cowls." He unfurled the hood of a friar.

"Escape?"

"If you wear the cowl no one will recognize you. Behind the chapel I have two burros packed with provisions. We can make our way south to Socorro, then to El Paso . . ."

Serafina imagined herself and the friar wending their way along the Río Grande in the snowstorm. Like Joseph and Mary fleeing to Egypt, leaving their homeland. Over them hung the wrath of Herod.

But she could not leave. Not that she feared the journey—no, for freedom she would suffer any hardship—but if she left, the four remaining prisoners would be sent as slaves to Zacatecas.

"I cannot," she whispered.

"How can I convince you the danger you face is very serious? Fray Mateo has been selected by the Custodian to bring the Governor to his knees. He will use you. If he can have you sent to the Holy Office in Mexico City, that will cause the Governor's downfall. Here brother will turn against brother, and you, in the middle, will have no one to protect you."

"I thank you for your kindness, but I cannot run away. Not until all the men are free." She reached out and took the friar's trembling hands in hers.

"I thought this would be your answer," he stammered, "but I had to act. You think only of helping others. You will be called a Joan of Arc, one who gave so much for her countrymen. I promise to stand by you . . ."

"Thank you, Fray Tomás," she whispered.

"May God be with you, my child." He made the sign of the cross over her and went out of the room, leaving Serafina alone.

Outside she heard doña Ofelia leave. When she was ready for bed she heard Gaspar take his post. She blew out the candles and slipped into the cold bed.

The winter storm swept down on the Villa de Santa Fé, obscuring the adobe houses of the hamlet. In the hills Serafina heard the call of a coyote, then an answer.

Even in the storm her father kept watch. She knew they would be camped in the hills, near the road that led to the northern pueblos.

The following morning the eighth prisoner was freed. Serafina returned to her room to work on her colcha, and the Governor and a squad of soldiers rode off, seeking the Apache band that had stolen a shepherd's flock near Galisteo.

When the Governor returned he met with emissaries from the pueblos. A few tribal leaders had come that day to tell the Governor they were pleased with his release of the prisoners. That evening he related the meeting to Serafina.

"Two of the caciques from the southern pueblos have come to visit. Chiefs from Isleta and Tiguex. They compliment me for releasing the prisoners. So, our bargain is working after all. I have you to thank for the goodwill we have garnered."

"I have played but a small part," replied Serafina. "And besides, the northern pueblos are not yet ready to compliment you."

"That is true. But I'm sure I'm on the right path. And I owe it to you. We have scared the Apaches away, and I feel I can relax. Now I can spend time with my horses—"

He looked at Serafina and wondered if she would ride with him. He was noted for his horsemanship, and he often thought that if he had sons or daughters they too would love horses as he did.

"Will you ride with me tomorrow?" he said impulsively. "I have a mare. Estrella is her name. She needs to be exercised, and I haven't had the time. We can go at a walking pace. It will be good for you to get some fresh air."

"What will the people say? The prisoner out riding with the Governor."

"Let them say what they will. I am the Governor, and I have every right to invite you. The hills will be snow-covered. Believe me, it will be beautiful."

Is he offering me a chance to escape? she thought. And am I ready? There is only one way to know for sure.

"Very well. I will go with you."

"You'll see how exciting a horse ride can be. Only the most trusted native auxiliaries who help us fight the Apaches are allowed to ride. I want you to feel the freedom, the joy. I'll have doña Ofelia bring you one of my wife's riding dresses."

He talked throughout the meal about his horses, and Serafina listened.

"I've talked too much," he said when the meal was done. "It's your turn."

Serafina smiled and began her story.

EIGHTEEN

The Native

This is the story of Trino, a young Indian from one of the northern pueblos. One day while he was hunting in the mountains he found a spring. Trino hid in the grass by the pool of water until he spied a deer that came to drink. He reached up and grabbed the deer by the leg. He tied a rope around its neck and led it home.

He locked the deer in a shed. The next day Trino took his knife and sharpened it. When he went to kill the deer, the young buck spoke to him.

—What are you going to do?

—I am going to kill you for food, replied Trino.

—Don't kill me. I am a prince that had a spell put on me. I was transformed into a deer. If you spare me I will give you a gift.

—What do you want me to do? asked Trino.

—Go to my father and tell him you found me and I am alive. He will try to give you money, but ask instead for the little mirror he owns. Bring it here and free me from this enchantment.

Trino traveled to the house of the father and told him he had found his son. The man offered money but Trino asked for the mirror. He received it and returned home.

—What do I do with the mirror? he asked the deer.

—Rub the mirror with your hands, replied the deer.

When Trino rubbed the mirror as he was told, a jinni appeared.

—I am at your command, said the jinni. Tell me what to do.

—Lift the spell from the deer and make him a man again.

The jinni obeyed and thus Trino was able to return the young man to his father. A great feast was held. Trino ordered the jinni to bring lots of posole, and so the feast lasted several days.

In those days there lived a king in the adjacent kingdom who promised to marry his daughter to the man who could build a bridge across the Río Grande. Trino heard of this and told his mother he was going to build the bridge and marry the princess.

—Don't go, his nana said, they might kill you.

—I will be safe, and I will return for you, Trino said.

So he journeyed to the king's palace and told the king he could build the bridge across the river.

—Many princes have tried, replied the king, and they failed. If you cannot build the bridge I will have you killed.

—Very well, said Trino.

—What equipment do you need?

—Only a pick.

The king and the people thought Trino was crazy. He went to the edge of the river and dug a cave. There he slept for many days. When he was rested he got up and rubbed the mirror. Instantly the jinni appeared.

—I am at your command. Tell me what to do.

—Build me a bridge across the river and a beautiful palace in the middle of the bridge.

When the king awoke that morning he saw a brilliant light coming from the river. He went to his wife and together with all the court they went to the river. When they saw the bridge and the palace they couldn't believe their eyes.

—You have kept your word, said the king, and he married his daughter Blanca to Trino.

Trino was very happy, but he didn't know there was a jealous prince who was in love with the princess. Prince Costa had spent all his money trying to build the bridge and had failed.

—I will have Princess Blanca for my own, he vowed.

He went to a witch and asked her help in discovering how Trino was able to build the bridge.

The witch disguised herself as a royal lady and went to visit Princess Blanca.

—Show me your bedroom, she said after they had had tea.

Princess Blanca showed her the bedroom. When the witch saw the mirror hanging on the wall she immediately knew it was special. Of course Trino had never told his wife about the mirror's power.

—What a beautiful mirror, said the witch.

—You may have it as a gift, said the princess.

The witch took the mirror to Prince Costa.

—With this mirror you can get rid of Trino, she said. The prince rubbed the mirror.

The jinni appeared.

—I am at your command, he said. Tell me what to do.

—Destroy the bridge and take the palace to a faraway place, said the prince.

And it was done.

That morning instead of awakening in his palace, Trino awoke in his cave by the river. There was no Blanca by his side, and no bridge. He rose and went to the king's castle.

By now everyone knew the bridge had disappeared. When the king heard the news he was very angry at Trino.

—The bridge you built was a fantasy! he roared. Now you must die!

—I accept my sentence, replied Trino, but first give me time to find my palace.

—You have one day, said the king. If you do not return in one day I will marry Blanca to Prince Costa.

A very sad Trino set out to find the palace that had disappeared. On the road he met an old woman.

—Where are you going? she asked.

—I am looking for the palace.

—Do you have faith?

—Oh yes, I pray to the Virgin Mary everyday.

—Then I will help you. A witch has stolen your mirror.

—What can I do? he asked.

—Down the road you will find a cat. Put it in your sack and take it with you. Then go back to the king's palace and tell the cooks you are a baker. Put your wedding ring in a cake and send it to Princess Blanca.

Trino did as he was told. He found the cat and put it in his sack, then he went to the king's palace. Preparations were under way for Princess Blanca to marry Prince Costa.

Trino went to the kitchen and asked the cooks if he could help bake the pastries for the wedding feast.

Trino baked pies and cakes. In one cake he hid his wedding ring, and he told the servants to take it to Blanca.

—Tell her to taste it right away. It's the most delicious one I've baked.

When Blanca cut the cake she found Trino's ring. She knew it was a message from Trino, and she sat down to cry. She did not want to marry Prince Costa, but she couldn't disobey her father.

One evil lady who watched over the princess immediately went to tell the witch that a cook had sent Blanca a ring hidden in a cake.

—Who is the cook? asked the witch.

—It is a native from one of the Indian pueblos, she replied.

—Aggggh! cried the angry witch. She knew Trino had returned. She had spent all her time secluded in her room, guarding the magic mirror. But now she had to act.

—Capture him! Capture him! she shouted. Throw him in the dungeon!

The guards shivered in horror. They knew the witch had filled the basement with rats. They were so hungry they would attack a man and kill him.

They had to do as ordered, so they seized Trino and threw him in the basement. Instantly the hungry rats jumped to attack him. Trino opened his sack and showed them the cat.

—Aiii! cried the rats. Don't let the cat loose! He will eat us up! Spare us, spare us!

—I will, said Trino, but you must go to the witch's room and bring back the mirror that hangs by her bed.

The rats went in a row, through holes in the walls, and they found the witch's room. She was sleeping, and they quietly took the mirror and delivered it to Trino.

Trino rubbed the mirror and the jinni appeared.

—I am at your command, he said. Tell me what to do.

—I want you to bring back my palace, bigger and more beautiful than before. Make the bridge wider and stronger. Take the witch who stole my mirror where no one will ever see her again.

As fast as a blink, everything he ordered was done. And as the sun rose the king looked out his window and saw the palace on the bridge.

—Look! he cried, the palace has returned. Is it real or a dream?

—It is real, said Blanca, and I do not have to marry Prince Costa.

They ran to the shining palace and Trino came out to greet them. Blanca was overjoyed to be reunited with her husband.

—How did this happen? asked the king.

Trino showed him the mirror.

—This is a magic mirror. Costa had the witch steal it from Blanca. Now it is rightfully returned to me. Ask me for anything and I will deliver it to you. I will protect you from your enemies.

The king was so happy he prepared a feast that lasted eight days. Trino brought his mother and introduced her to Blanca and the king. It is said they lived happily ever after.

As for Prince Costa, he disappeared, and no one has heard from him since.

NINETEEN

The Governor was laughing heartily by the end of the story.

"That's a wonderful story! And you have placed the story along the Río Grande, with a Native as the protagonist. How creative. Is this happening? Are the cuentos being shared by the people?"

"Yes," replied Serafina. "The stories are being shared. Doesn't it make sense that we should put some of our men as heroes in the stories?"

"Yes, it does. It makes complete sense. This sharing of the stories could be the best thing that has ever happened to us. Do the Españoles appear in your legends?"

"Yes," said Serafina, "but not often as heroes."

"Ah, I see." The Governor nodded. "There's the rub. We see ourselves as heroes, but others don't. Well, Trino's story is delightful nevertheless. Now you must rest. Tomorrow we ride."

He walked her to the door and wished her good night. Doña Ofelia appeared and led her to her room, and as soon as the old woman was gone Serafina went to bed.

The cry of coyotes in the hills lulled Serafina to sleep. She dreamed horses of many colors, but then the images shifted and she saw a burning castle, heard the cries of people. In the distance the Governor rode away, carrying with him a tattered flag, the banner of Governor don Juan de Oñate.

The following morning la Villa de Santa Fé awoke to fresh snow on the ground. Chidren rushed out to play in the snow, followed by their barking dogs that also frolicked in the white powder. Smoke poured from chimneys, lending the fragrance of burning piñon and cedar to the air.

Hardy men left their homes to milk cows and collect eggs in the hen houses. Determined hunters headed for the hills to hunt. The snow would drive the deer herds into the lower cañones.

In spite of the snow, or maybe because of it, a spirit of joy seemed to infuse the inhabitants. Yes, it was cold and the adobe huts were difficult to keep warm. The winter provisions, which consisted of deer and buffalo jerky, corn and wheat flour, were running low. Still, they welcomed the cleansing snow, the promise of moisture it brought to the fields.

A few of the residents gathered to observe the trial. Most knew the ninth prisoner would be set free, but what drew out the Governor's enemies was the gossip. Last night the Governor had dinner with the Indian woman, they whispered.

"A disgrace!" one man clamored. "Consorting with the enemy is an act of treason!"

Treason! Those who hated the Governor repeated the word. Now they could use his relationship with Serafina against him. He was not carrying out his duties to protect the colony, they said. It was this faction that had reported the Governor's actions to the agent of the Inquisition in Santo Domingo.

Wrapped in buffalo robes they stood huddled in front of the porch. The storm had passed, and even though the temperature hovered below freezing, the New Mexican sun shone brightly. By noon it would be warm enough for the men to cut firewood and for the women to visit their neighbors.

The four remaining prisoners were led forward, then the Governor appeared. Smiling, dressed in stylish cotton pantaloons, white shirt, and a leather jacket, he cut an imposing figure.

He asked for the charges to be read against the man from Picuris, listened to the defense, and then pronounced the man free. Murmurs of dissension were whispered by his enemies as they moved away. The Governor took no notice. When the prisoners passed by him he stopped Serafina.

"Are you ready?" he asked.

Serafina glanced at the snow-covered hills, their slopes dotted with green junipers and piñon trees. Beyond those hills, a few hours' ride by horse, lay her pueblo.

"We will go at a walking pace," he added. "It's safe."

"I have only to change into the riding dress," she answered.

"Gaspar will escort you to the horses," said the Governor. "We will ride within the hour." He strode toward the corrals, whistling a tune.

As Serafina turned to follow the guard she spied a crestfallen Fray Tomás standing alone in the middle of the plaza. He looked at her with resignation, then walked back to the chapel.

Within the hour, Gaspar and Serafina appeared at the corral behind the Governor's residence. Juanito, the stable boy, had finished tacking up. The Governor's two dogs, eager for the excursion, chased each other around the corral, agitating the Governor's already nervous stallion.

The Governor smiled when he saw Serafina. She looked as beautiful as any Spanish lady in the riding dress. More beautiful. Her bronzed beauty seemed to emanate from the land itself.

"You look lovely, señorita," the Governor gallantly greeted her.

Gaspar frowned. "Will that be all, Your Excellency?" he asked.

"Yes, Gaspar. Thank you."

Gaspar glanced at Serafina, then walked away. He would have given his right arm to be the one riding with Serafina. But he did not have the authority of the Governor, and he didn't even own a horse.

"Come," the Governor said, holding out his hand. "It's quite safe. Juanito will hold the mare. You mount from this side. Use this bench. There. Now foot on stirrup, and up you go."

He handed her the reins. "Hold this tight. Don't pull. The mare is well trained; she knows what to do. If she decides to move from a walk to a trot, you can hold her back with the reins."

"I understand," Serafina replied, and the Governor mounted his steed, a nervous red stallion that pranced and snorted and swirled in a circle.

"They're eager for the run!" exclaimed the Governor, exuberant and clearly happy that Serafina had agreed to ride with him. The fresh snow on the ground, the morning air crisp and the sun shining brightly, the scent of burning wood in the air, the fragrance of the horses, all the senses responded and seemed to come alive.

"Ready?"

"Yes."

The Governor nodded and the stable boy opened the gate. Out they went, the horses trembling with excitement, plumes of frosted air exploding from their nostrils. Their snorting and whinnies were answered by other horses kept in the distant pastures.

Frowning eyes followed the exit of the Governor and Serafina as they rode out of the villa and up into the hills. How dare he ride with the Indian girl! A prisoner! Leaving the business of the colony unattended! The viceroy in Mexico City would hear about this. Many harsh letters condemning the Governor and asking for his removal would be in the mail when the oxen-drawn caravan went south that spring.

The Governor noticed nothing. This morning he was full of joy.

"The land holds magic," he cried, smiling.

"Yes," replied Serafina, getting the feel of the mare, pulling softly on the reins to see how sensitive a tug was needed for her to respond.

"There's no view of the world like the view from a horse," said the Governor. All his life he had been a horseman, a caballero. In distant times he would have been a knight.

The Governor's horse pranced and snorted, its muscles and sinews bulging with power, eager to run. He made the stallion rear up and turn smartly on its hind legs.

"See this wide arroyo," he pointed at the cañada that ran down between two hills. "It's sandy and clean. Very good for a run. I'm giving my horse its rein for a quarter mile. You wait here. The mare will try to follow. Hold her back tight."

With that he spurred the stallion and it bolted forward, thrusting its power into the run it had awaited since they left the corral.

The mare whinnied and started forward, but Serafina didn't hold her. She pressed her legs into the soft flanks and the mare quickly went from a canter into a full gallop. The wind tore Serafina's black hair free, and for a moment she felt the freedom she hadn't known in days.

The Governor turned, startled at first, thinking the mare had been spooked and would throw its rider. He pulled his horse to a stop and yelled, "Olé! Cuidado!"

But Serafina pressed the mare, clearly not holding on but racing with expertise. She passed the startled Governor who recovered and gave chase.

Up the cañada they raced, the pounding of the hooves raising clods of sand and snow, the stallion and the mare breathing heavy, the sound of their bodies filling the silence.

Serafina let out a loud cry, a piercing cry of war. *Free at last* her long, joyful cry seemed to say. At the end of the cañada lay a path into the foothills, a path she knew well. There would be a camp there where her father and other scouts waited. They would hear the horses, and they would be ready.

The Governor, too, raced, afraid Serafina would be thrown from the mare. But quickly he realized Serafina wasn't in danger. She was an expert horsewoman. Where had she learned to ride like that? Native women were not supposed to know how to ride. This did not bode well.

"Stop!" he cried, and still Serafina raced on, the mare hot and thundering under her, as glad to be running as her rider.

The Governor spurred his horse, but already the heavy stallion was winded. In a few minutes Serafina would leave him far behind.

They were almost at the end of the wide arroyo when Serafina held up and brought the mare to a stop. The surprised Governor rode up panting, not knowing what to say. She sat on the mare like a warrior, her black hair falling around her shoulders, breathing hard.

They looked at each other in a new way, as two who had shared something special. She was his equal on horseback, an ability he admired.

"You ride well," said the Governor.

"I could ride all day, but I think the mare has thrown a shoe. She started to limp on her right foreleg."

The Governor alighted and helped Serafina down. Then he lifted the mare's foreleg and checked the shoe. The shoe was fine, the hoof clean. He had not seen the mare limp, still he checked the other hooves.

"Everything's in order," he said, drawing a deep breath. He looked at the end of the wide arroyo. There at the top of the incline lay the road to the northern pueblos. He thought he saw a man move in the rocks at the top.

He turned to Serafina. She was looking in the same direction.

"Perhaps it is a sore ligament," he said.

"Yes." Serafina nodded, breathing hard, a sheen of perspiration on her face.

"Let's go back at a walk," he said.

He turned his horse and she followed, walking their horses slowly back toward the villa.

As they rode, the Governor wondered again where Serafina had learned to ride. Had the mare really come up lame, or had

Serafina stopped her? He knew that in a few minutes she could have escaped.

The snow sparkled on the hills. The piñon and juniper trees dotted the hillsides, and above them rose the majestic Sierra Madre, the mountains the setting sun turned red as the blood of Christ. Clouds gathered on the peaks. Perhaps it would snow again. In the meantime the evergreen trees seemed to loosen their scent and their fragrance filled the air.

Content with the beauty around them, the two rode into the plaza.

That evening, when Serafina returned to have dinner with the Governor, doña Ofelia noticed something different in their relationship. Yes, the Governor was as polite as ever, but he seemed more relaxed. And Serafina kept her usual poise and noble bearing, but she did not seem so much on her guard, so distant.

Ah, thought the old woman as she served dinner, the Governor is deluded if he thinks he has found a daughter. Serafina will return to her pueblo. She will never become a Castillo.

Dinner ended and Serafina sat in a chair in front of the fireplace. The Governor sat across from her as she began her story.

TWENTY

Belda and the Beast

here was a man who had three daughters. Two were mean and so wasteful they spent every penny their father had. Belda, the youngest, was kind.

That summer the father received a summons, demanding that he appear immediately in the city to settle his debts. When he was leaving, he asked his daughters what gifts he could bring them.

The two eldest daughters asked for many expensive presents.

—If you pass by a garden bring me a flower, Belda said.

The poor man saddled his horse and hurried to the city to answer the summons. It was late by the time his business was completed and he had bought gifts for his two eldest daughters. On the way home it grew dark, and he lost the way. Spying a light in the forest, he followed it and was surprised to find a wonderous palace hidden in the trees.

He put his horse in the stable and entered the deserted palace. In a huge dining hall he found a large table set with all kinds of food. He ate supper and fell asleep.

In the morning the table was set for breakfast; he ate and went out to saddle his horse. As he was passing through the garden he stopped to admire the beautiful flowers.

—Dear Lord, he said, I had forgotten that Belda asked me for a flower. He reached out and cut a rose.

At that moment a huge, horrible beast appeared.

—For taking my flower, I am going to kill you and eat you, roared the beast.

The frightened man fell to his knees.

—Don't kill me, cried the man. I have three daughters who depend on me. At least allow me to go and tell my daughters I must die.

—I will let you go, replied the beast, but I must have one of your daughters instead of you. Go and ask your daughters which one wants to die in your place. I'll give you eight days to return with her. Take this bag full of gold coins as a gift to them.

Sadly the man took the bag, got on his horse, and hurried home. When he told his daughters what had happened, the two eldest daughters were only interested in the money.

It was Belda who spoke.

—I will gladly die once and a thousand times for you, father.

So it was decided, and on the eighth day Belda and her father traveled to the beast's palace. The place was deserted, but the table was set with delicious dishes. They ate and rested and at eight o'clock the beast appeared.

—Have you chosen to die in your father's place? he asked.

—Yes, replied Belda. She was not frightened of the beast.

The father was sent away, and Belda was led to a bedroom where she slept. The following day she spent the day alone, wandering about the palace. In the afternoon she found the table set with food and was eating dinner when the beast appeared.

—You're not afraid of me, are you?

—No, Belda replied.

—May I stay and watch you eat?

—Will you join me? she asked.

—No, I will only watch. I want to hear all about you.

Belda told him all about herself, but the beast revealed very little of his past.

Eight days passed, and each day the beast would come and sit with her while she ate. The beast was falling in love with

Belda, and her admiration for his kind ways and pleasant conversation was also turning into love.

On the eighth day he asked her if she was sad.

—I am not sad when I am with you, she replied. But I grow sad because my father and sisters think I am dead, and yet I am enjoying everything in this palace.

—Would you like to visit your family? asked the beast, knowing that if he let her go he would die.

—Oh yes, said Belda.

—Will you marry me? he asked.

—I cannot till I speak to my father.

—Put on this magic ring, he instructed. It will take you to your loved ones. But don't forget me; if you do I will die.

—I will never forget you, Belda said. I have grown to love you while I have been here. But I do want to see my family.

She put on the ring and in an instant she found herself back home. Her father was overjoyed to see she wasn't dead. He wanted to know all she had done at the palace and how the beast had treated her.

—Were you happy there? her father asked.

—Yes, she replied. I fell in love with the beast. He said if I forget him he will die. What should I do?

—It must be the poor beast is under some kind of enchantment, her father said. If you truly love him, then you must return to him.

She closed her eyes and saw the beast sitting in the flower garden. He looked sad, and she knew he was dying. She ran to her room, put on the ring he had given her, and instantly she was by his side.

—Belda, he whispered, you've returned.

—Yes, she replied. When my father asked me if I was happy with you, I realized I was happier here with you than ever before. I will marry you.

The minute she said these words the evil spell was lifted from the beast. He was a handsome prince that had been enchanted by an evil sorcerer.

—Only the love of a maiden could free me, he said. I will take care of you forever.

—And I will love you forever, replied Belda.

TWENTY-ONE

"Ah, a story of the beauty and the beast," murmured the Governor. "A delightful children's story. I heard several versions when I was a child. The prince has been enchanted; he is a frog or an ugly monster, and only the princess's kiss can lift the spell."

He looked thoughtfully at Serafina. Am I the beast? he thought. Has the difficult life in this godforsaken kingdom of la Nueva México made me a beast? I go to church, I confess my sins, I listen to music. I have read the few books in my library, I am a civilized man.

But the prince, too, was a civilized man once upon a time. What incantation turned him into a beast? And why? I don't believe in such things, but perhaps we all have the capacity to be beasts. Yes, that's it. Even an enlightened man can turn away from goodness and beauty and become a beast.

Perhaps my life as a soldier turned me away from beauty. I am constantly on guard against the Apaches and the Pueblos, and so I have forgotten to see the beauty of the land and the people. Now, through Serafina's eyes I see beauty again.

"Why does Belda fall in love with the beast?" he asked. "After all, he is hideous in all aspects, and she doesn't know he is an enchanted prince. Is true love blind?"

Serafina smiled. "Love is not blind," she replied. "On the contrary, it can look deep into the souls of those we love. True love doesn't look at the surface; it looks within."

"So a beautiful person can fall in love with an ugly person?" said the Governor.

"There is no such thing as ugliness," she replied. "We believe every person has a place in nature."

"Beauty is in the eye of the beholder," mused the Governor.

"Nature is not ugly," Serafina said. "Everything has its purpose."

"It is we who name this person ugly and that one handsome. But isn't there a consensus on what is ugly and what is beautiful?"

"Not in my world," replied Serafina.

An interesting notion, thought the Governor as he leaned back in his chair. As Cervantes belittled the writers of knightly love with his Quijote, each one of us can choose not to join the crowd that labels one person ugly and the other beautiful.

"Everything in nature has a purpose," he said, "and nature does not make ugly things." He looked at Serafina. "But the story tonight was so short. Can you tell me another story?"

"Some stories are short, but they may carry the importance of one of the longer novels on your shelf." She glanced toward the Governor's books.

The Governor rose and picked up the book. "Ah, the adventures of don Quijote. Written by a man who would have understood your philosophy. My mother taught me to read. She loved fables, fantasies, and romances. Here I read to free myself from the pressures of the day. Your stories do the same."

"Yes, some stories provide a respite, a rest from the day's work," she agreed. "We have stories about tricksters that make us laugh. But your cuentos seem to be more of a mirror in which you see yourself."

"Yes, the stories are mirrors," said the Governor.

"Now I must excuse myself," said Serafina, rising. "Tomorrow the priests from Santo Domingo will question me."

The Governor frowned and also stood. All evening he had kept at bay the nagging predicament. He didn't want Serafina to fall into the hands of the Inquisition, but he was helpless to stop the interview.

"You know I must let them question you. I could run them out of the villa and quote the law that says the natives are not subject to the Inquisition. But that would only serve my enemies. They would raise a cry of protest. I believe it is better to let them ask you a few questions, satisfy themselves, and that will be the end of the matter."

"I understand," Serafina replied, and in her tone the Governor wondered if she was blaming him for allowing the agent of the Inquisition to question her.

He reached out and took her hand. "Trust me, the session will be short. If I refuse to let them interview you it could be the final rift between the civil and religious authorities. It would split the colony. I can't allow that. I must walk a tightrope. I have made it clear to Fray Mateo that you are my prisoner. I will keep you out of their clutches."

"I trust in your judgment," Serafina answered, weighing his words carefully. "Now I must wish you a good night." She bowed and left the room, leaving a very perturbed Governor mulling over the choice he had made.

The next morning a cold wind blew in from the north, sweeping gray clouds over the mountain peaks, threatening another storm. A sullen mood pervaded the trial of the tenth prisoner.

The charges were read, the defense presented, and the Governor freed the man. Now only two prisoners remained, Serafina and a man from the pueblo of Taos. The Taos man was escorted back to the stockade, and the Governor motioned for Fray Tomás to bring Serafina forward.

"I will accompany you to the interrogation," he said, and she and the friar followed him into the Governor's residence.

Early that morning doña Ofelia had lit a fire in the fireplace so the room was warm. Two young friars, members of the committee sent to interrogate Serafina, stood by its warmth. The third, Fray Mateo, sat at the table. He rose to greet the Governor.

"Good morning, Your Excellency. Thank you for your hospitality, but we would have preferred to interview the prisoner at the church. In these matters it is best—"

"Good morning, Fray Mateo," the Governor interrupted. "You and your assistants are my guests. As I explained to Fray Tomás, I insist that the questioning be done here. I have agreed to this interview as a matter of courtesy. There is no one in the villa who thinks the girl is guilty of a crime that merits the attention of the Inquisition. As you know the young woman and the men were arrested under my authority. But even those charges are being dropped for lack of substantial evidence."

The Governor's demeanor drew the ire of the wrinkled and stern friar Mateo. "On the contrary," he countered, his voice harsh and commanding. "We have the written testimony of witnesses that leads me to believe that we are dealing with a very dangerous heretic."

His cold look penetrated Serafina's calm demeanor, and she shivered.

"Please sit," he commanded, and Serafina took a seat at the table. The two friars hurried to take seats opposite her. One took up a quill pen to record the proceedings.

The Governor scoffed. "A dangerous heretic? The young woman known as Serafina? I have known her for some time, and I assure you, there is nothing heretical about her."

Fray Mateo stepped to the table and lifted a sheath of papers. "We have the written testimony of witnesses—"

"What are the accusations?" exploded the Governor, losing his patience. "Witchcraft? That's nonsense. Fray Tomás has questioned the girl and found her innocent. Tell them, padre!"

A nervous, cowed Fray Tomás stepped forward and mumbled, "Yes, I questioned the girl. I absolved her. She attends mass, she knows all the prayers . . ." He stumbled and looked for understanding from the two young friars. They remained quiet, but Fray Mateo spoke up.

"Fray Tomás may be well meaning, but he is inexperienced. There are many ways the Devil tempts the weak."

"Yes," agreed the Governor, "the Devil works in many ways, perhaps even by clothing himself in the robe of a friar. But there are no specific charges here, and my hospitality is growing thin. Serafina is my prisoner. I am in charge of deciding if the Devil has tempted her or not, and I will not have her falsely accused to satisfy your whims."

"These are not whims!" shouted Fray Mateo, striking the table. "There are specific charges the church commands me to investigate through the Holy Office of the Inquisition!"

"What are those charges?" asked Serafina, and all turned to look at her.

Fray Mateo's lips parted in a thin smile. "Your father is the leader of a clan. The clan uses the cactus fruit called peyote. Your people consider the peyote to be a god. They speak to it as if were a god. The reports I've read say the peyote brings you visions. These are visions from the Devil. We have a witness that swears you have participated in those pagan rituals."

The Governor looked surprised. This was an accusation he had not expected. Yes, he knew the natives held many secret ceremonies, and among them the use of peyote was the one the friars worked to stamp out. Peyote induced visions, so the friars had labeled all such practices the work of the Devil. As far as the church was concerned, the practice was the most heinous form of devil worship.

Fray Mateo loomed over Serafina. "You must acknowledge that you have participated in such ceremonies where the Devil was present! You must denounce the Devil! But first, you must denounce your father for his use of peyote!"

"I denounce the Devil, but I will not denounce my father!" Serafina replied.

"Do you admit your father takes part in rituals where the peyote is ingested?" shouted the friar.

"The ceremonies of the clan are none of your business," replied Serafina.

"You must answer the question! Have you taken part in such rituals?"

"Of course I take part in rituals of my clan, but—"

"There! She has confessed!" cried Fray Mateo, looking around the room triumphantly.

"But we do not worship the Devil as you say," answered Serafina. "We pray as our ancestors taught us to pray."

"You should pray to the saints," commanded the friar.

"The saints are your ancestors, and we honor them. Your saints are like our Kachinas. We pray to the saints at church, and we have our ceremonies to honor the Kachinas."

Fray Mateo shook his head. Changing his tactic, he lowered his voice and placed a hand on Serafina's shoulder. "My dear child, you cannot pray to the saints and to your pagan gods in the same breath. We know the friar at your pueblo taught you the catechism of the church. There is only one God. You must renounce all the false gods of your people."

"I cannot renounce my ancestors," replied Serafina. "I cannot renounce the cloud people who bring rain to our fields, or the Corn Mothers who sustain us. I have become a Catholic according to the teachings of the friars, but I keep the path of my people."

"If you do not renounce that path, as you call it, I have no choice but to conclude you are under the spell of the Devil." Fray Mateo turned and looked at his two young assistants. "Do you agree?"

Both glanced at Serafina then nodded.

He turned to the Governor. "I must remove the young woman to Santo Domingo, where we can conduct a full hearing, with witnesses for both sides, and—"

"I forbid it," the Governor interrupted.

"You can't," sputtered the friar.

"I forbid Serafina's removal from my jurisdiction. Until she is tried under my authority she remains my prisoner."

Fray Mateo had suspected the Governor would fight the removal of the girl, but the Governor was playing it safe. By insisting the girl must first be tried by the civil authorities he had won the legal argument. At least for the moment.

"Very well," answered Fray Mateo, acknowledging the Governor's finesse, "you have a point. When is her trial date?"

"Day after tomorrow," replied the Governor.

"Then we shall wait," said the friar, looking at Serafina and smiling. "Once you have tried her and she is released you have no further jurisdiction over her. Then it will be our turn. I am sure Fray Tomás will grant us the hospitality of his residence for two days. We will wait. Come," he said, and the two friars at the table gathered their papers and followed him.

"Good day, Your Excellency," said Fray Mateo as they swept out of the room, an embarassed and wistful Fray Tomás following in their wake.

"Damn him!" the Governor cursed as the door shut. "What impudence! What ignorance!" He controlled his anger and turned to look at Serafina. "Forgive my words of anger. But the actions of friars like Mateo only serve to drive your people to insurrection."

"Perhaps they have already created a gulf which a bridge cannot span," she replied.

"What do you mean?" asked the Governor.

Serafina sighed. "Perhaps our worlds are already so divided that only—" She paused and looked into the Governor's eyes. "If a father treats his son as a slave, the son will revolt."

What is she saying? thought the Governor. That the revolt we fear is imminent? That my freeing the prisoners as an act of goodwill is too late? That the natives will no longer bear the rule of the father? I am the father, I am the civil authority.

"Is it too late?" he whispered.

Serafina did not answer.

"Poor child," he said, He took her hands and she rose. "You are tired. You must rest. One thing you must believe, I will not hand you over to them."

He looked at her and realized how much she had come to mean in his life.

"You should rest. And don't trouble yourself with this matter. You are safe as long as you are with me."

He called for doña Ofelia and the old woman appeared at the door.

"Ay, Dios mío," doña Ofelia whispered as they made their way to Serafina's room, "what a day. The cold chills my bones. I am old, and the old smell death. It hovers over the villa like a shadow. The Indios say they have seen the Virgin floating on a cloud. A woman dressed in blue, they say. She has come to tell the Españoles to leave this land. What are we to do?"

She paused at the door. "I fear for you," she told Serafina, and Serafina saw worry etched on the face of the old woman. "I will pray that the good friars do not take you away." She turned and disappeared.

Serafina took up her colcha and began to stitch. Outside, the wind moaned and tore at the mud roof of her room. Vigas held latillas on which dirt had been packed. With the snow the dirt grew wet and heavy, and leaks appeared.

In the hills wolves called, their mournful cries frightening the horses in the corrals behind the Governor's residence.

A strange power was loose in the world, nature's warning.

Why do they want me to leave my church, the way of my ancestors? Serafina wondered. *Am I the lamb to be sacrificed? Do they want to make a lesson of me? Don't they know that such a trial would be the spark that ignites the wrath of our people against their rulers?*

That day not even the hardiest souls stirred from their homes. Blizzard winds blew over the villa, making travel impossible. The howling wind drove the snow into drifts, and the villa seemed to disappear from the face of the earth.

That evening when Serafina joined the Governor for dinner she could tell he was trying to be joyful. Doña Ofelia had swept and dusted every corner, and she had prepared a special dinner, a broiled turkey and sweet empanadas. Dozens of candles burned, their smoke scenting the room.

"We must endure the storm," the Governor said as he greeted Serafina. "We need the snow; it has been so dry. Maybe this means the drought is breaking."

All through dinner he masked his true mood by relating affairs of state, plans for laying new irrigation ditches, a new road, and a grand scheme for uniting the pueblo natives against the marauding Apaches that constantly swept down on the Native and Hispanic villages.

"The Apaches are our common enemy," he said. "They raid your villages and ours. They steal our children, drive off flocks of sheep, destroy our corn fields. If we can unite against this enemy, we can survive."

He talked about his plans as if he were talking to a trusted confidante, sharing his ideas and plans with Serafina. But when dinner was done he sat back, took out a cigar and made himself comfortable.

"Ah, it has been a long day," he said. "Tell me a story."

TWENTY-TWO

El Picaro

In times long past there lived a princess who never laughed. She was beautiful, but she was always frowning. No one, not even her parents, had ever seen her laugh.

One day the king asked the queen if she had ever seen their daughter laugh.

—No, replied the queen, she didn't laugh as a baby, nor when she was growing up.

—Now she is eighteen and many suitors have come to ask her hand in marriage. If there is a man who can make her laugh, I will allow him to marry her, the king proposed.

So the king prepared a grand fiesta, and he sent out an invitation for everyone in his kingdom to attend. Young men came dressed as jugglers, acrobats, comedians and clowns and tried to make the princess laugh, but they all failed.

On the third day of the fiesta Lino, a young man with few skills, was walking by the palace. At the palace doors many vendors had set up stalls to sell their wares. One vendor was selling beautiful walking sticks.

—May I see one? asked Lino.

—Get away from here you rascal! shouted the vendor, and he struck Lino a blow on the back.

—I may be a picaro, but I'm honest, replied Lino.

He escaped into the palace, where he learned the king was looking for a man who could make the princess laugh. Lino decided to try his luck.

The king had set up three doors through which the partici-pants had to pass. At each door stood a gatekeeper.

—Let me pass, said Lino to the first gatekeeper.

—Whoever performs for the princess gets one hundred pesos, said the gatekeeper. I'll let you pass if you give me 25 per-cent of what you earn.

The dishonest gatekeepers were obviously making a lot of money from those they let enter.

—Yes, Lino agreed, I'll give you 25 percent of what I earn.

He went through the door and met the second gatekeeper. He too wanted 25 percent of what Lino earned, and Lino agreed. The third gatekeeper asked for the same, and Lino said yes.

The king was disappointed when he saw Lino. He would never marry his daughter to a worthless young vagabond.

—Picaros are not allowed to perform, said the king. Just take the hundred pesos and leave.

—Your royal highness, I don't want the hundred pesos, replied Lino.

—Well, what do you want?

—Instead of the money I want you to beat me one hundred times with a stick.

The princess who was standing nearby heard the strange request and smiled. The young man asking to be beaten seemed so serious, she couldn't help but giggle.

—What do you mean you want a hundred blows? asked the angry king.

—That's what I want. Please do me the favor.

The princess had never heard anything so outlandish. She cov-ered her mouth to keep from laughing, but the king and queen saw her. This was the first time they had ever seen her smile.

—Very well! shouted the king. Tie him up and give him one hundred blows! And make them hard, he whispered to his guard. I don't want this rascal married to my daughter.

—Wait, your highness, said Lino. I have some friends, and I promised them a share of whatever I earn. May they come in?

—Bring them in, replied the king.

Lino went to the first gatekeeper and told him to come and receive his share of the earnings.

—Here is my friend who will recieve 25 for me, Lino told the king.

—Is it true? asked the king.

—Yes, said the gatekeeper, not knowing the 25 he was about to receive were blows.

—Very well, said the king. Tie him up and give him his 25.

The dishonest gatekeeper was given the beating of his life and sent packing. The lords and ladies of the court laughed heartily. They realized Lino had tricked the gatekeeper. The princess, too, was laughing.

Then Lino called the second gatekeeper, and he too came in, expecting to receive 25 pesos.

—Are you ready to receive 25 for this young man? asked the king.

—Yes, replied the gatekeeper, and they tied him to the post and beat him 25 times.

Lino did the same with the third gatekeeper. He received 25 blows and went away grumbling.

By this time the princess and the others realized the trick Lino had pulled on the dishonest gatekeepers. The young rascal knew how to take care of himself, and the king would have to keep his promise.

—There are still 25 blows left, said the king to Lino. Are you ready to receive them?

—Please allow me a few moments, replied Lino, running out of the palace.

Lino ran out to the stall of the man selling walking sticks.

—What do you want? asked the mean merchant.

—The king owes me 25 sticks. Why don't you buy them?

—Are they very expensive?

—I'll sell them to you for 25 pesos, Lino replied.

That's a bargain, thought the merchant.

—Are they good sticks?

—Yes, they are very good. If they give you one you don't like say you didn't like it, and they will give you another one. In this way you can have all 25.

If these are the king's sticks they must be very good, thought the crooked vendor. I can sell them for twice the money.

—Very well, he said, here are your 25 pesos. Now let's go collect my sticks.

They went into the palace where everyone was waiting. When the princess saw the eager vendor she knew Lino had tricked him, and she laughed harder than before.

—Your highness, said Lino, this man has come to collect the 25 you owe me.

By now the king was also smiling. The rascal was bright, capable of handling any situation. And his daughter seemed to like him.

—Is it true? asked the king. You have come to receive the young man's 25?

—Yes, said the greedy vendor. I paid 25 pesos for those sticks. But I bought them on condition that they be good sticks. You have to give me good, solid sticks that I like.

—Tie him up and give him 25, said the king.

They tied him and the guard delivered the first blow.

—Did you like that one? he asked.

—No, I didn't like it, groaned the vendor.

—Well then, here's another one. The guard struck a second blow.

—Did you like that one? asked Lino.

—Yes, I liked it! cried the vendor.

—Well give him more, said Lino.

Everyone saw the vendor couldn't win. If he didn't like the blow, he got another one. If he liked it, he still got another. When all 25 blows had been struck the vendor said he had learned his lesson. He crawled away vowing not to be dishonest.

The king kept his promise, and Lino married the princess. Later Lino became the ruler of the kingdom, proving that a clever rascal can outwit those who are dishonest.

he Governor chuckled. "A wonderful story," he said, filling his wine glass. "By his wits the rascal gets the princess. In our culture the picaro is a well known character. In this case his craftiness punishes the mean vendor and the greedy gatekeepers. I like it. Tell me, do you have such characters in your stories?"

"Our picaros are usually animals," replied Serafina. "There are many stories in which an animal, like the coyote, plays a trick on other animals."

"Stories about picaros usually teach us a lesson," said the Governor.

"And they make us think. For example, I've often wondered about the three gates in the picaro's story. What do they represent?"

"I never thought of them as having a deeper meaning," replied the Governor. This was a talent he admired in Serafina. She probed into the meaning of the cuentos. In the past ten days the stories she had told had taught him a great deal about himself.

"Perhaps there are three doors to arrive at heaven," she said. "The friars teach us St. Peter guards one of the doors to heaven."

"Or the passage of life," said the Governor. "The first door is a passage from childhood to young adulthood. The second door represents the responsibilities of work, marriage, family. The last door is death . . ."

He paused. Yes, there was some hidden symbolism in the three doors.

"And the princess who never smiled? Does she stand for a certain type of character trait? Is she afflicted by melancholy?"

"Perhaps," replied Serafina.

"But why? She lives in a palace; she has everything she needs."

"But in all the cuentos of your people, the king is very powerful. It is he who decides when to marry his daughter, and to whom."

"That is our custom. A family needs a strong father. The king is not only the daughter's father, he is the father of the nation."

"Perhaps the princess needs her freedom. Having the father and later the husband decide everything for her doesn't allow her to blossom. She will never know what she's capable of accomplishing."

The Governor raised an eyebrow and thought. Was Serafina sad? Was she the princess pining for freedom?

"Are you sad?" he asked.

"I miss my family," she replied. "But from childhood we are trained that life is difficult. We do not dwell on sadness."

"I see. You say the princess won't know what's she's capable of doing. Do you know your capabilities?"

"Yes, your excellency. When I was a child I was given a vision."

"And what is that vision?"

"To free my people."

The Governor sighed. The joyful mood he had cultivated all evening suddenly grew cold. The humor in the story drifted away. They seemed to be where they started, he on one side of the fence and she on the other. He respected her as a person and a storyteller, but even his admiration for her was not enough to solve the enmity between her people and his.

"Will you follow your vision?"

"I must, Your Excellency. If one doesn't follow one's vision one hurts the community. I cannot disappoint my people."

"And the princess in the story—if she had a vision, what would it be?"

"She would need to find something that she could do well. She must ask herself, why am I not happy?"

"Why do you think she was unhappy?"

"Perhaps there was no love in her life."

"So she fell in love with Lino, the picaro."

"Yes. Apparently the young men of the court did not interest her. Lino is different. He breaks through her silence."

"Yes. Not laughing is a silence." He paused. "You never laugh."

"A prisoner has little to laugh about," replied Serafina. "Even in the king's palace."

"Yes." The Governor nodded. "I understand, and yet I cannot change the situation."

He knew Serafina needed her freedom, but he could not set her free.

"Perhaps I am as much a prisoner as you," he whispered.

She nodded. "I have learned that in your culture every profession makes a prisoner of the person. The higher in rank the more you must obey the rules of your profession."

"And I, as governor, am bound by many rules and regulations," mused the Governor. "Well, you have given me much to think about. But the immediate issue at hand is saving you from Fray Mateo. I am sure the encounter with the friar was not pleasant for you. I am selfish for taking so much of your time, but you know the evenings with you mean more to me than I can say."

He thought of asking her for another story, but he knew the rules. Instead he said, "It is time for you to rest."

"Yes," Serafina said, and rose.

The Governor went to the door, opened it, and called for doña Ofelia.

"Good night, Serafina. Do not worry yourself about Fray Mateo."

"Good night, Your Excellency. May your dreams be peaceful."

"Yes, yes don't worry," doña Ofelia muttered as they walked to Serafina's room. "They threaten to take you before the Inquisition and you are not to worry. Ay, bless the Governor, may he find a way to save you from their clutches."

Serafina said good night to the old woman and entered her room. It was too early for bed, and besides, there was much to think about. She picked up her colcha. Stitching allowed her mind to review the day's events.

The interview with Fray Mateo had not gone well. He was a crafty interrogator, and if they took her to Santo Domingo she would be no match for him. Would the Governor be there to be her protector?

She shook her head. Being fearful would not help her people. What mattered were the plans to free themselves from the rule of the Castillos. She didn't know how that would come about, but she guessed Popé was already back in Taos making plans for a revolt. He hated the Españoles and would do anything to drive them from the land.

She thought about the meetings she had attended with her father in her own pueblo. Sitting in the kiva late at night, the men discussed the harsh rule of the Españoles. Each night the representatives from the different pueblos came closer to advocating an open revolt.

What would it mean? Could the Pueblo people return to a way of living they had known before the Castillos came? Could they forget the language and all the friars had taught them? Could they live without the tools the Castillos had brought?

A knock at the door made her look up from her work.

"Who is it?" she asked, knowing doña Ofelia never knocked. Was the Governor returning? The door opened enough to reveal Gaspar.

"May I come in?" he asked in a voice so plaintive Serafina could not refuse him.

"Yes, come in."

He entered and softly closed the door behind him. He stood there, hesitantly. His curly blond hair framed a flushed but handsome face. He was probably eighteen, a young man already toughened by life in the frontier colony of la Nueva México. It was clear that he had no knowledge of a way with women.

"Good evening, Gaspar."

"Good evening. I hope you don't report me to the captain. I know it's against the rules to visit a prisoner."

"I won't report you. What is it you wish?"

"I'll only stay a few minutes," he stuttered. "I hope you don't think it is improper of me, a simple soldier in service of the Governor to wish to talk to you. By that I mean—"

He stopped, feeling confused. He had dreaded the act of knocking on her door. Standing in front of this beautiful young woman he felt like a bumbling fool.

"I consider you a gentleman, Gaspar," said Serafina, smiling and attempting to put him at ease.

"You do?"

"Yes."

"And I truly respect you in the highest . . . I am not accustomed to . . . I have never approached a young woman, such as yourself, with the motive of expressing my . . . how shall I say this so you do not think that I am taking advantage of you. . . ."

"You have only to speak freely," Serafina suggested.

"Thank you for allowing me that courtesy. You know that I have only the highest regard for you. The same respect I bear for my parents and God."

"You are very kind, Gaspar. You have been most respectful in your duties, and I appreciate that. You are a gentleman, and I trust you."

"I only wish my parents could have the honor of being here with me. I have told them how much I admire you. My mother has sent you a gift, hoping you will accept it."

He came forward carrying a pair of buckskin tewas.

"Will you accept them?"

Serafina took the tewas. It was clear they were fine Cochiti moccasins, woven with pieces of turquoise tied in a row up the side. The leather was soft, worked to feel like cloth by the woman who made them.

"They are lovely. Yes, I accept them."

"My mother said the feet of a princess should not go cold in winter," he explained, his face beaming at her acceptance of his gift.

"I thank your mother, but I am not a princess."

"That's what some are calling you."

"And the others call me a witch."

Gaspar frowned. "Those are the people who want to keep your people subjugated. They accuse you of witchcraft as a means of keeping control over you. They cannot understand why you do not ask for freedom for yourself. My parents have been to all the trials. We are in complete agreement that all of you should be set free. Your people and mine must find a way to live together."

"I wish that were so," said Serafina.

"May I call you Serafina? It is a lovely name."

"It is my Spanish name, not my Indian name. Yes, call me Serafina."

"What is your Indian name?"

"I cannot say."

"Forgive me. I shouldn't have asked. I dreamed I could speak to you, tell you what's in my heart . . ."

"You are free to speak."

"I came to propose a plan to save you," he whispered.

"What is the plan?"

"That you marry me. Do not take me wrong," he said hurriedly. "But if you marry then Fray Mateo cannot take you to Santo Domingo. I am volunteering. If you marry me you would be a free woman. My parents have agreed to go to your pueblo. They will speak to your parents. I assure you, it will be very proper. My parents are farmers like yours. When I finish my soldiering, I too will farm. I am single, and strong."

He stopped short, breathless, afraid his proposal would be such an insult that she would call for doña Ofelia.

So the young man thinks he can save me from Fray Mateo by marrying me, thought Serafina. How noble of him.

"I thank you, Gaspar, but—"

"I will abide by your decision. I, too, am a man of honor, even though I am a lowly guard. But if you accept my proposal of marriage it will make you a rightful citizen in the eyes of the church."

Gaspar believed their marriage would not only save her, it would improve the relations between the Españoles and natives. And during the past ten days he had fallen in love with her. Together with his parents they had formulated this plan.

"I fear marriage will not stop Fray Mateo," she said.

"The Governor will help us," replied Gaspar. "He loves you like a father. He will send the friar scurrying back to Santo Domingo."

"You are so confident."

"I have fallen in love with you," Gaspar replied. "Whatever your decision I will abide by it."

Serafina smiled. "I will think of your offer as a gesture of concern and—"

She was interrupted by a sound at the door.

"I must go," Gaspar said, turning to open the door. He was greeted by doña Ofelia carrying a cup of hot chocolate.

"What are you doing in here?" said the old woman, her eyes piercing Gaspar. "A guard should be on duty! Don't you know your place? Outside! Outside!"

"Sí, señora," the startled Gaspar mumbled, scurrying around her and out of the room.

Doña Ofelia looked at the tewas Serafina held, shook her head then placed the cup of chocolate on the table.

"He brought you a gift," she said, turning to Serafina.

"He proposed marriage," replied Serafina. "Out of concern for my safety."

"Yes, I'm sure he means well," said Doña Ofelia, taking the tewas and looking at them carefully. "He comes from a good family. And these are well made. Probably cost him a sheep or two. Ah, the ideas young men get in their heads. What did you tell him?"

"I thanked him."

Doña Ofelia nodded. "There is only one who can save you, the Governor. He has the power." She handed the tewas back to Serafina and said good night.

"Thank you for the chocolate," Serafina relied. "And for the advice."

The old woman shrugged and went out, leaving Serafina to ponder a new option. What if she married Gaspar? She would then be the wife of a Castillo, and her place in the society would be different. Some of her people had learned so much of the Castillo's culture they no longer returned to the pueblo way.

She shook her head. I cannot contemplate fantasies, she thought. I have to keep to the course my father and his neighbors have set for the people.

Serafina slept fitfully; nevertheless, she was up at sunrise, offering prayers to the sun that blossomed over the Sierra Madre peaks, its light streaming through cracks in the east wall. A thin ray of light cut across the middle of her face as Serafina prayed.

She took the small bag of corn pollen doña Ofelia had given her and offered a pinch of pollen to the light.

Then after a breakfast of corn meal and a tortilla she followed Gaspar outside. He glanced to see if she was wearing the tewas, and when he saw she was, he smiled.

The freeing of the eleventh prisoner went quickly. A cold wind blew from the north, but those gathered at the ceremony did not hurry back to their warm homes. They stood transfixed, watching not the man who was set free, but Serafina.

Now only she remained of the twelve, and tomorrow it was her turn. The trials would end tomorrow, and all present could not help but wonder what it would mean. Would the Governor's pardons settle the ill feelings of the natives? Or was the gesture too late?

Serafina spent the day working on the colcha. It was nearing completion, but she did not feel satisfied. A loneliness she had not felt before crept into her heart. Now she was alone. Yes, her stories had freed her fellow men, the Governor had kept his promise. But what now?

Perhaps the same mood infected the Governor, for when she entered the dining area for the evening meal, she found him staring into the fire at the fireplace.

When he turned to face her a sigh escaped his lips.

"Good evening, Serafina," he said, taking her hand and leading her to her chair. "Doña Ofelia tells me you are almost finished with the colcha."

"She has been most helpful," replied Serafina, "Bringing me pieces of cloth and thread. And she has taught me new stitches, so it is a bedspread that will last you long after I'm gone."

"You made it for me?"

"Yes, it is a gift. For the kindness you have shown me. For freeing the men."

"I will accept the colcha with many thanks," said the Governor. "In it I will wrap my dreams."

"May they always be pleasant dreams," she replied.

"Yes, but truthfully, it is you who freed the prisoners. Your stories have struck a chord in my heart."

Serafina nodded. "Your people seem to be very emotional. You cry when a family member dies. You show much emotion on Good Friday. I have seen the friars and men flagellate themselves. And, as I understand, you have so many expressions for love."

"Yes," said the Governor. "There are many ways to express love and its emotions."

"Do emotions also come from the books you read?" she asked, looking in the direction of the shelves.

Ah, what a thoughtful question, thought the Governor. "Yes, stories in books stir our emotions. A book can cause joy, anger, despair, or hope. A book can stir patriotism or revolution. Just like the cuentos you tell stir my emotions. What do you feel when you tell stories?" asked the Governor.

"I feel I am passing on knowledge," she replied.

"Have you ever felt love?" he asked.

"Yes. I feel love for my people."

"What about my people?"

"I feel kindness for those who are kind. But to give kindness one must recieve kindness. Love thy neighbor, as Christ taught. Now there is so little kindness we are losing hope."

"Yes, you're quite right. And so it is our duty to bring that kindness into our lives."

He understood it was by no accident Serafina had been delivered to him. Her stories had helped him reflect on his situation. Stories give knowledge, she said. And he had learned a great deal. Now he had to save her from the Inquisition. But how could he save her when he was the one who kept her prisoner? He could not be two persons in one.

"Shall I tell you a story?" Serafina asked, breaking the strange revery he had fallen into.

"Yes, that would please me very much."

"Since I go on trial tomorrow, perhaps this short tale of an Indian lawyer would be appropriate," she said, and she began the story.

TWENTY-FOUR

The Native Lawyer

fter many years of not seeing each other, two friends met at a village fiesta. Manuel invited Rufo to come to his home for breakfast the following morning.

—I will come if you let me buy the eggs, said Rufo. He insisted and gave Manuel twenty-five pesos to buy a dozen eggs.

Manuel bought the eggs, and the next morning his wife boiled them for breakfast. They waited a long time for Rufo to arrive, and finally decided he wasn't coming, so they ate the eggs.

Manuel didn't feel right about eating the eggs his friend had paid for, so he went out and bought a dozen eggs.

—Put these eggs under one of our hens, he told his wife. When the chicks are born we won't sell them, and when they are chickens and lay eggs we will raise more chicks. Half of everything that is produced from this dozen eggs, I will give to my friend Rufo.

A dozen chicks were born and when they were grown they began to lay eggs. Manuel sold some of the eggs and set the money aside. The rest of the eggs he allowed to hatch. Soon he had the most thriving business in the country. And always, he put aside half of his earnings to give to Rufo.

With the money he made from the egg business he bought many ranches, cows, and sheep. He became the richest man in the entire Río Arriba region of the Río Grande valley. He told everyone that all his riches had come from the eggs Rufo had given him, and when he saw his friend again he would give him half of everything he had earned.

Finally the news reached Rufo that Manuel had grown exceedingly rich, and that everything he had earned came from the eggs he had bought for breakfast long ago. He saddled his horse and rode off to visit Manuel.

—I am glad to see you, said Manuel. Do you remember the twenty-five pesos you gave me to buy eggs? I bought them and boiled them, but since you didn't show up for breakfast my wife and I ate them.

—How did you become so rich? asked Rufo.

—I bought another dozen eggs, and from those I made a fortune. I made a promise that I would give you half of anything I earned.

Rufo shook his head.

—If all this wealth came from the money I gave you, then everything belongs to me.

Manuel was surprised.

—That's not fair, he replied. I've worked hard to accumulate this wealth. I'll give you half and that way both of us profit.

—No, said an angry Rufo, it all belongs to me! And if you don't sign it over to me I'll take you to court!

Rufo went off in search of a lawyer. He found two who said they would represent him in a suit if he gave them half of all he was awarded by a judge. Rufo agreed and the two attorneys brought a suit against Manuel.

Soon the entire region was talking about the case. Everyone thought Rufo would win. Manuel tried to find a lawyer who would represent him, but none were willing.

One day as he sat contemplating his fate, Salvador, an Indian neighbor who lived in a nearby pueblo, walked by.

—How are you, vecino? asked Salvador. You look very sad. Tell me, what's the matter.

—There's too much to tell, replied Manuel, and nothing you can do to help.

—I'm your neighbor, maybe I can help.

—What I need is a good lawyer, but I can't find one. Tomorrow I have to appear in court. I'm afraid I'm going to lose everything own.

—How did this happen? asked Salvador, and Manuel told him the entire story.

—Oh, compadre, I think I can persuade the judge to rule in your favor. How much will you pay me?

Manuel was surprised. How could an uneducated Indian win his case?

—I would pay you fifty pesos.

—No, that's too much. Give me a bushel of corn.

—If you win you deserve more, said Manuel. Thank you, neighbor.

—Oh, and bring a pot of cooked habas, those beans I like so much.

Manuel thought that Salvador wanted the beans for lunch, so the following morning he was ready. When Salvador arrived he wrapped the pot of fresh baked beans in a serape and off they went.

The courthouse was packed with people. Everyone wanted to know if Manuel had found a lawyer to represent him, but they saw him arrive with only Salvador at his side.

—Is he your attorney? a man asked.

—Yes, answered Manuel.

Everyone laughed, thinking the Indian could never beat Rufo's two educated lawyers.

When the judge entered he looked at Salvador and shook his head. He asked Manuel if he had a lawyer.

—Yes, replied Manuel, Salvador is my attorney.

Laughter broke out again. Salvador had lifted the lid from the pot and was eating beans. An illiterate Indian eating beans could hardly be a good attorney.

The judge banged his gavel and called for the first of Rufo's lawyers to present his case, which he did very eloquently. Then the second lawyer rose and finished by saying if all of Manuel's fortune came from the eggs purchased by Rufo's twenty-five pesos then the fortune belonged to Rufo. When he had presented the argument he sat down.

All the time Salvador was dipping into the pot and eating beans.

—It is your turn, don Salvador, said the judge sarcastically.

—Father Judge, said Salvador, I ask the court to lend me a piece of land so I can plant a crop.

—Is that all you have to say? asked the exasperated judge.

—Oh, I have to ask Manuel what he did with the eggs he bought with the twenty-five pesos?

Manuel rose and said,

—My wife boiled the eggs and we ate them.

Then Salvador asked Rufo if he had told Manuel to prepare the eggs for breakfast.

—Yes, replied Rufo. I told him to cook the eggs for breakfast.

Salvador turned to the judge. I ask your honor to lend me a piece of land to farm.

—The court is not in the business of lending farmland! exclaimed the judge. I'm tired of you asking the silly question. Is that the only defense you have?

—Yes, your honor. I can only ask the court to lend me a piece of land to farm.

By this time the judge had decided the Indian was crazy, and so it would be best to humor him.

—And what would you plant on the land? he asked.

Salvador reached into the pot and pulled out a handful of beans.

—I would plant these beans, he said.

—You are crazy! replied the judge. Those beans won't grow! They've been cooked.

—Yes, said Salvador, just as the dozen eggs Manuel bought with the money were boiled. Nothing could come from those eggs.

The surprised judge nodded. Salvador had made his point.

—What you say is true. No further product could have come from the boiled eggs, and so I must rule that Manuel keeps his property. The court is adjourned.

Manuel went home with his good neighbor Salvador, leaving everyone in awe of the native lawyer. His common sense had beaten the educated lawyers.

TWENTY-FIVE

"So," said the Governor, "some of our cuentos are beginning to have a native influence. I like that. Salvador is not the ignorant indio the judge makes him out to be. He has an inbred sense of justice and figures out how to illustrate a point in the law."

"Perhaps I need Salvador as my attorney," replied Serafina, smiling.

"Don't you think Capitán Márquez has served well as a defense lawyer?"

"What would have happened if my friends had relied solely on Capitán Márquez?"

"You have a point," said the Governor, rising to pace slowly around the table. "I really don't know how I would have ruled. Still, I'm convinced I've done the right thing."

"I agree, Your Excellency."

He paused at the fireplace and turned to Serafina. "If Salvador were your attorney, how would he defend you?"

Serafina closed her eyes. The flickering light of the candles played on her face, illuminating her beauty.

"Perhaps he would say I'm like a tree uprooted from its native land and brought to a place where it doesn't know the soil. The tree might thrive for awhile, but eventually it will die."

Serafina's answer pierced the Governor's heart. His dream that someday she could be his daughter, or like a daughter, was just that, a dream. She had just said that she could never live in the culture of the Españoles.

"You are that tree," he whispered.

"A wounded body can go on living and hope to recover its health. But a wounded spirit is a different matter."

"Your spirit needs to be rooted in your pueblo."

"Yes, that is the center of my world. My spirit needs the teachings of the ancestors. Just as you need your church, I need mine."

"But you, and your people, have learned to live within our church. You have learned to use our language, our tools, and all of this has been to your benefit."

"We have learned to survive," Serafina answered, "but our spirit cries for a renewal of our tradition. We must hold the Kachina dances without interference."

There it is, thought the Governor, as always. Their traditions and ceremonies create the deep split between our cultures, and the root of our problems.

"Ah," he whispered, "if only I could pass a law that would solve our differences, bring peace to our land."

"Why can't you?" asked Serafina.

He looked at her and felt his shoulders slump.

"Impossible. Laws passed have to be approved by the Viceroy in Mexico, the Council of the Indies, the king . . . It is a complex legal system that governs all of us. Such a law would involve the church . . . no, it's impossible."

Serafina rose and went to the Governor. "I understand your role as governor is not an easy one. I thank you for freeing the men. You have done the right thing. The leaders at the pueblos will consider this a goodwill gesture on your part. But truthfully, I don't know if it will solve the discontent we feel. So much more needs to be changed, and as you say, you and the friars do not have the power to change the laws that bind you."

"The laws that bind," the Governor repeated, taking her hands in his. "As you said last night, we are bound by the professions we chose."

Serafina felt his anguish, but there was nothing she could do. She was the prisoner, and long before she satisfied her own desires she had to keep in mind the freedom of her people.

"I must go," she whispered.

The Governor nodded. "Tomorrow is your day."

"Yes."

"Are you going to cook a pot of beans?" he said, smiling, trying to cloak with humor the serious situation they both faced.

Serafina returned his smile. "Or bring a shovel so I may be planted here and take root."

"Yes," the Governor said. "A tree may be transplanted and take root. The fruit trees and grape vines our ancestors brought from Spain have taken root and thrived. Las rosas de Castillo bloom in every home. Their blossoms beautify the spring days in all our valleys. Perhaps the earth was foreign at first, but it's earth nevertheless."

"Still, a tree is not a woman," she said sadly. "Good night, Your Excellency."

"Good night, Serafina."

"Pleasant dreams," she said at the door.

"And for you—" The door closed and she was gone.

Because of the worry in her heart Serafina did not sleep well that night, awakening to a morning that dawned clear and cold. She said her prayers at sunrise, then bathed herself with the hot water doña Ofelia brought in a pan. She tied her hair in braids, the chongos some of the women of the pueblos wore. Then she dressed in the dress she had worn the day she was taken captive.

"I washed the white gown," doña Ofelia said as Serafina ate the breakfast of atole and tortillas.

"Thank you, but today I prefer to wear my own clothes."

"I think I am more nervous than you," the old woman said, scurrying around, checking this and that. "Imagine, today you are a free woman. Don't forget me when you return to your home.

Ah!" she exlaimed, picking up the Serafina's colcha. "But I thought you had finished."

"No," said Serafina.

"Look here. The corner you had finished is undone. Who would have—"

She looked at Serafina. She had unraveled her own work. Why?

"I didn't like it," Serafina said simply.

"But isn't it a gift for the Governor?"

"Someday I will finish it," Serafina said in a tone that told the old woman she would explain no further.

At that, Gaspar knocked on the door. It was time to deliver her to the trial.

Doña Ofelia touched her handkerchief to her eyes. "You've been like a daughter to me," she whispered, following Serafina outside. She had not attended the previous trials, but today she felt the girl needed her at her side.

In his office the Governor paced back and forth, pausing to open the door a crack and peer outside.

"Dear God," he whispered. It seemed as if the entire villa had turned out for today's trial. The plaza was packed. Women in their Sunday clothes gossiped, the men smoked their pipes and discussed the pros and cons of the Governor's actions, children scooted through the crowd, chasing each other in a game of tag, dogs barked.

The young men of the villa sat on their horses on the west end of the plaza, eagerly awaiting the appearance of Serafina. The nervous mounts quivered and snickered, prancing and turning with excitement. They snorted at the crisp morning air which carried the scent of horses in the corrals, and they whinnied, eager not for the trial but for the excitement of a run.

Under the portal, don Alfonso, the secretary and notary, had already set up his table and journals. He was ready to record the trial of Serafina as he had recorded those of the previous prisoners, but he too felt the uniqueness of the day as he looked out over the crowd.

The Governor saw don Alfonso whisper something to Capitán Márquez. Behind them stood Fray Mateo and his two assistants, ready to cart Serafina off to Santo Domingo as soon as the Governor freed her.

Then Serafina passed by and the Governor watched her take her seat at the table. Capitán Márquez leaned to say something, and she shook her head.

Ah, what regal bearing, thought the Governor. She is like a queen and we her mere servants.

"This will be a difficult day," he whispered, and felt his heart pounding in his rib cage. Why do I hesitate? he thought. Is it Serafina who is on trial today? Or I?

Taking a deep breath, he opened the door and stepped out on the portal. All turned in his direction, and a silence came over the crowd.

A strange thought passed through the Governor's memory. He remembered riding in a rainstorm one day. A bolt of lightning had hit nearby, sending a deep, tingling sensation through his body. He felt a similar energy coursing through his body, a feeling created by those who waited for him, and by the serene look in Serafina's eyes.

"Good morning, ladies and gentlemen," he said, breaking the spell. "It is a beautiful day."

He looked toward the eastern foothills, and all followed his gaze.

"We have snow in the mountain, perhaps more will come and break the drought. Let us thank the Lord."

He bowed his head and all did likewise. Silence filled the plaza, broken only by the bark of a dog, the low mooing of a cow that hadn't yet been milked, the cry of two magpies that suddenly alighted on a tree at the far end of the plaza. Then all was silent again until the Governor spoke.

"Today we are gathered for the trial of the young woman known as Serafina. Her Indian name has not been revealed to us. According to the custom of her people she chooses not to tell us that name, and we respect her wishes. So, for all time she will be known simply as Serafina. Don Alfonso," he said to the secretary. "Will you please enter the young woman's name in your record and read the charges."

Serafina stood to hear the accusation read.

The secretary scribbled Serafina's name and the date in the leather-bound ledger, then read the indictment. As with the prior prisoners, Serafina was charged with planning a revolt against a colony of his royal majesty.

"Capitán Márquez," the Governor said, nodding. "Will you present your defense."

The captain stepped forward. "Your Excellency, the prisoner has requested that she be allowed to offer her own defense."

A murmur of surprise floated through the crowd. The secretary started to protest but the Governor cut him off.

"You may present testimony on your own behalf," said the Governor, looking at Serafina. "But are you sure you don't want Capitán Márquez to present a defense?"

"The captain has very ably represented the other prisoners," replied Serafina, "and because of that they are now free men . . ."

Capitán Marquez acknowledged the compliment with a nod.

"The prisoners freed know how to speak the language of Castile, but not well enough to stand before a judge and defend themselves. I have been schooled in your language," said Serafina, "and so I am capable of defending myself."

The Governor nodded. "True, you are very capable in our language. I see no reason why you should not present your own defense. But please be advised that the charges are serious. Are you willing to take the chance that you might not succeed in your defense?"

Another slight murmur rose from those assembled. The Governor was challenging her.

"Let the girl defend herself," cried a man from the crowd, and the majority of those assembled took up the cry. "Yes, let her speak."

Even the Governor's enemies took up the cry. Yes, let her. Let her fall flat on her face. She had no training in law. Let her be sentenced and carted off to Santo Domingo to face the Inquisition.

The Governor held up his hand and asked for silence. "I am not averse to having the young woman represent herself," he said. Turning to Serafina he nodded. "Very well, proceed."

Serafina rose and looked at the audience, thankful for their support, aware also that a small antagonistic faction only wished her failure.

She had some knowledge of the people of the villa. During days of fiesta the people from the pueblos came to trade their corn, turkeys, and vegetables for the iron pots, pans, knives, axes, and buffalo robes.

Serafina had often visited the villa with her family, and so she knew the character of the Españoles, those they called Castillos. They were shrewd traders, but for the most part honest, hardworking people. On those days of fiesta there seemed to be no animosity between the Españoles and the natives. An air of goodwill filled the plaza as the people traded goods and visited with their neighbors.

The young people especially enjoyed the respite from work. The young men raced their horses around the villa. Single young women strayed away from their parents to watch the horsemanship.

After the races the young riders went to the river to water their horses, and they talked with the girls from the pueblos.

There were few young women in the villa, so the boys enjoyed flirting with the Native girls.

There were a few pleasant memories in this mixture of cultures, thought Serafina. But now time and its consequences weighed heavily on her.

"Your Excellency," she began. Then turning to the gathered crowd she spoke to them.

"Ladies and gentlemen, as you count on your calendar, eighty-two years ago your Governor Juan de Oñate first came with your ancestors to our land. Our people welcomed your ancestors. They had no home, they were tired and sick after their long journey. They had no food. At San Juan they were allowed to settle. Our people, of this valley you call Española, helped your ancestors by giving them corn and buffalo robes. Our people helped build homes and churches. Some of your ancestors took wives from our pueblos. We learned to speak your language and to use iron tools. You planted wheat to make tortillas; we learned to eat bread made of wheat.

"Now your ancestors are buried in this land. They have gone to your heaven. They rest in peace. But our ancestors do not rest in peace. They know that the friars do not allow us to conduct our ceremonies as we have from the beginning of time. Those strict rules of the friars are the reason we come to you and ask for relief."

Here Serafina paused and looked at Fray Mateo. His face was as stern as a granite cliff. Fray Tomás, on the other hand, nodded, as did others in the audience who were in sympathy with the natives.

A small group of elders from the pueblos stood huddled on the south side of the plaza. They listened carefully to her words, but they showed no expression.

"You have a law that says we must give to the civil authorities part of our corn crop each summer. That leaves our storehouses empty during the cold winter. You have a law that states our men must work in your fields during the summer. True, they are paid, but it means we can grow less to feed our families. During farming season many of our men must work building churches, so our fields go fallow.

"All this we have borne for eighty-two years, but we can bear it no longer. What you call religion is important to us. You think our religion is evil, but it is not. It is a way to honor our ancestors, to honor the cloud people who bring rain. Our ceremonies keep us alive."

Fray Mateo jumped to his feet. "What the girl is describing is paganism. That is precisely why we abhor their ceremonies. They pray to masks and fetishes. They dance half naked during their Kachina dances. The church has sworn to stamp out such practices. No, it is not the friars at fault here. The natives insist on keeping their pagan ways. The girl has confessed as much."

The Governor too jumped to his feet. "The accused is explaining the circumstances as she understands them. She has confessed to nothing, and I thank you not to interrupt the proceedings!"

Fray Mateo mumbled a protest and sat back down.

"You may continue," the Governor said to Serafina.

"I am accused of following the ways of my people, and to that I confess," Serafina said.

The crowd stirred uneasily. Most did not want the poor girl to hang herself with a confession. They only wanted her freed like the previous prisoners, so the tension the arrest of the twelve had created could be put behind them.

"But I have also learned your religion, and I pray to the Jesus and the Virgin. I pray to your saints."

"That is not enough," Fray Mateo mumbled. "You must renounce your pagan gods."

"This is a civil trial," said the Governor sternly. "If you interrupt again I am not above sending you in chains back to Santo Domingo!"

The crowd drew back in surprise. The Governor was being very forceful. Such an act would send vibrations all the way back to the Viceroy in Mexico City; indeed, to the king himself.

Fray Mateo glared at the Governor but said nothing.

"We must keep our ways if we are to survive as a people," Serafina continued. "You know that we meet to discuss this problem. You know the elders of our pueblos have gone to the friars many times, seeking relief. I stand accused of meeting with the elders of my pueblo to discuss how best to bring the injustice we feel to your attention. Because I speak Castellano like you I was to be a representative of my people. I confess to that."

A sigh of confusion flowed across the crowd. Had she confessed to plotting revolt?

Only Fray Mateo smiled at her words. As far as he was concerned immediately after the trial he could start back to Santo Domingo, taking the girl with him.

"But you must know," Serafina continued, raising herself up to her full stature, projecting her voice to the farthest corners of the plaza. "You must know that a storm of protest is gathering in the pueblos. This is not a secret. Our elders, those we call our holy men, have seen the signs. Our ancestors speak to our elders. They say this is our land, and we must continue holding our ceremonies and dances as we see fit. If you do not listen to our elders, you will bring the storm upon yourselves. This is all I have to say."

She sat and a hush came over the crowd. The scratching pen of the secetary stopped. In the alamos a raucous crow called, a dog barked. A woman or two in the crowd touched handkerchiefs to their wet eyes. The men who recognized the truth in

Serafina's words shifted uneasily from one foot to the other. It seemed an eternity before the Governor stood.

"We know what Serafina says has some truth to it," he said, looking out at the crowd. "But we also know that we have come to this land to bring civilization and the word of God. Our faith is very strong. Our desire to make this land our home is no longer contestable. As the prisoner has stated, we have been here eighty-two years. Our children and our children's children have grown up here. In our cemeteries rest our parents and grandparents. Shall we renounce our history in this land?"

The crowd shook their heads. No, they could no longer give up their homeland, the kingdom of New Mexico. Life was difficult, the drought had created a near catastrophe, the old feud between the civil authorities and the church continued, and recently the attacks from the Apaches menaced the colony.

The mission settlements along the Río Grande had become their homeland. Those colonists whose ancestors had come with Oñate no longer had any other place to call home. A few Españoles and criollos constantly arrived from New Spain to join the colony, and so the colony grew.

A woman in the front of the crowd acknowledged this by shouting, "This is our home. We have no place to go."

"We must make peace with the natives," someone behind her shouted.

"Peace with those friendly to us," a harsh voice cried, "but death to those who plot revolt!"

Dissension spread through the crowd, neighbor arguing against neighbor, until the Governor raised his arms and called for quiet.

"This is a point of great concern we cannot settle in one day," he said when the crowd quieted down. "My task here today is to conduct a trial."

"Ay," said the secretary as he raised his pen to write down the judgement. "And how do you find the girl?"

The Governor looked at Serafina, and she at him.

"I have listened carefully to Serafina's defense," the Governor said so softly those in the back of the crowd could not hear him.

"We cannot hear the judgment," someone in the back shouted. "What says the Governor?"

Then the Governor spoke loud enough for all to hear. "I say the young woman known as Serafina has met with a group of natives who discussed revolution. She must remain in my custody until such time as I am convinced that she is no longer a threat to the well-being of our colony."

Serafina's gaze had not left the Governor's, nor did her expression change as he voiced his decision. She seemed to feel the inner turmoil that he felt, but she stood poised and calm as if she had expected the outcome.

The secretary looked with surprise at the Governor. "What?" tumbled softly from his lips. Had he heard correctly?

Fray Mateo started to stand to protest, then slumped back into his chair.

"You win for now," he whispered to himself. If the Governor kept Serafina his prisoner the friar could not take her to Santo Domingo for trial.

Gaspar stood with open mouth, turning to look from the Governor to Serafina. Fray Tomás made the sign of the cross and bowed his head. Capitán Márquez looked puzzled.

Everyone thought they had not heard the correct verdict.

A cold breeze rustled across the plaza. The natives who had stood at the far end of the plaza quietly made their way out of the villa.

"Do you wish me to enter a guilty verdict?" asked the secretary.

"Write that she remains in my custody," said the Governor.

A murmur went up from the crowd. They had heard correctly. the Governor was not releasing the girl. What could this mean?

Turning to doña Ofelia the Governor ordered her to take Serafina to her room.

The old woman nodded, then took her shawl from her shoulders and placed it around Serafina. Together they walked past the Governor.

As Serafina passed in front of him the Governor felt like reaching out to touch her, to assure her that he had made his decision in her best interest. He wanted to let her know that only he could protect her.

He tried to smile, to let her know his thoughts, but the moment was awkward. He yearned for some sign from her, some token of understanding, but she gave no indication of her feelings. As royal as a princess she held her head high and disappeared with doña Ofelia into the Governor's residence.

EPILOGUE

There are probably a thousand and one cuentos preserved in the folklore of New Mexico and its vicinity. I have chosen twelve of these folktales to translate from Spanish into English. The cuentos were brought by colonists from Spain into Mexico (then called New Spain) and later into New Mexico. Here, they have been told and retold by the descendants of the colonists since 1598.

Listening to the stories as a child I learned the value of our oral tradition. The cuentos are not only a form of entertainment, they are also instructive. They preserve the Hispanic community's folkways, values, and traditions. We are fortunate that excellent folklorists such as Juan B. Rael and Aurelio Espinosa collected our rich store of cuentos. In their books the reader will find the telling of the folktales in our New Mexican Spanish.

If you are not familiar with our cuentos you may wonder why in the distant colony of New Mexico stories of kings and queens appear. Remember, our cuentos came from Spain, but the original tales originated in the subcontinent of India and centuries ago made their way into Persia, then to Europe.

Most often the folktales kept their original characters, and so kings and queens appear in the cuentos of New Mexico. But as the cuentos were told the storyteller adapted them to the New Mexico landscape and to the people. The Spanish becomes the Spanish of the Nuevo Mexicano. Some characters and plots from the Pueblo Indian world can be found in a few of the cuentos.

It is important for the reader to know something of New Mexico history. In August 1680 the Pueblo Indians rose up in revolution and drove all the Spaniards and their loyal Indian allies out of New Mexico. Many friars and hundreds of Spanish colonists were killed, as were many Pueblo Indians during the intense fighting. Finally the Spaniards fled the capital, la Villa de Santa Fé. They settled in the El Paso area and returned in the reconquest of 1692–93, led by don Diego de Vargas.

After the 1680 revolution, it is said, the returning Spanish friars and colonists realized the Pueblo Indians had the right to freedom in practicing their religion. A peaceful coexistence of cultures began to take hold in New Mexico. As time went on, there was more intermarriage between the cultures, creating a unique blend sometimes called Indohispano. The descendants of the original Spanish colonists call themselves Hispanos or Nuevo Mexicanos. The Pueblo Indians identify themselves according to their particular pueblo and language.

In 1848, the war with Mexico ended, and a large part of northern Mexico, including New Mexico, was ceded to the United States. Anglo American traders who had been trading with the New Mexicans began to settle in the territory. Today these different cultures, each with its own language and culture, live in a multicultural setting.

The Pueblo Indian revolution was the most successful Native American revolt against a European colony in the history of our country. It has much to teach us about colonial New Mexico and about relationships between different cultures. Taking this historical information as inspiration, I created the setting for Serafina's stories. The Governor I created for this story is fictional. The actual governor of New Mexico at the time was Otermin. This is not Otermin's story.

There are other points of information the reader might find helpful. In the Hispanic cuentos many of the characters don't have names. I gave them names for the sake of clarity. The cuentos have been passed down in Spanish in the oral tradition for centuries, so the story and its context were well known to both storyteller and listener. That ambience is hard to recreate on paper, so I took liberties in filling in spaces, adding or deleting this or that detail. My translations follow the plots of the stories but they are not literal.

What of the colcha, the blanket Serafina was weaving? Some say it still exists, perhaps in the museum in the Palace of the Governors in Santa Fe. Others say it was taken back to her pueblo. I wrote *Serafina's Stories* in the first years of the twenty-first century. Could the colcha have survived for over three hundred years? Wouldn't it be wonderful if we found her colcha so we could verify Serafina's existence?

There is another whispered part of the legend that tells us Serafina later married and had many children. Perhaps we are all Serafina's children, and that is why we continue to tell stories. I wrote her story to honor her as a spiritual great-grandmother from our New Mexican past.

I believe there is inherent power in the stories of our ancestors. Folk tales began in the imagination eons ago, and they nurture our creativity today. We recognize the values and concerns of the people in the folktales. Serafina told cuentos brought to New Mexico by the Spaniards. In her own pueblo she would have told the stories of her people. Understanding and respect for other cultures can begin by learning their stories.

The harsh treatment of the Pueblo Indians by the Spaniards is documented. Colonialism has never been easy on indigenous populations. A revolution did occur, and it happened because the Pueblo people sought to throw off an opressive government that threatened their cultural and spiritual existence. Not all of the Pueblo Indians joined the revolt; some remained friendly to the Spaniards and actually fled with them to El Paso. For a better understanding of the period it is important to read the history of the time.

Eighty-two years after Oñate's colonists settled in New Mexico the Pueblos revolted. As I interpret history, the main grievance at the root of the rebellion was the Pueblo Indians' insistence on keeping their religion, the ways of their ancestors, their Kachina dances. It was only a matter of time before a spark ignited a rebellion, and that spark may have been the harsh punishment imposed by Governor Treviño (a real governor who served from 1675 to 1677) on forty-seven Tewa Indians. When those leaders from the pueblos plotted revolt he punished them severely. But even before Treviño's action there are accounts of previous smaller revolts by the Pueblo Indians. The response to any act of revolution by the Spanish Governors was often harsh.

When de Vargas returned to resettle New Mexico the Spaniards had learned that in order to coexist they had to be more tolerant of the Pueblos' religious practices. The Pueblos lost much of their original land, but even in their smaller reservations they kept alive their languages and ceremonies. Today the Pueblos exist as sovereign nations within the United States.

There are so many social, political, and religious issues to study in this important era of New Mexico history. When a culture as distinct as the one the Spaniards brought to New Mexico in 1598 met the unique indigenous cultures of the Pueblos, conflict was sure to take place. What could those in charge have done to pave the way for tolerance and understanding? What could they have done to prevent the bloodshed of revolution? Perhaps its easier to judge history than to know the motives and actions of those who actually lived in that time.

Different cultures are still meeting on the world stage, and because of lack of tolerance and understanding those differences often explode in violence. Perhaps by studying and understanding the history surrounding the 1680 Pueblo Indian Revolt we learn not to place blame, but how we can live together in mutual respect. As a wise man said, we cannot change history, but we can learn from it.

Rudolfo Anaya
Alburquerque, New Mexico